Economic Value and Ways of Life

T5-BQB-791

Edited by
RALF ERIKSSON
MARKUS JÄNTTI

Avebury

Aldershot • Brookfield USA • Hong Kong • Singapore • Sydney

Published by
Avebury
Ashgate Publishing Limited
Gower House
Croft Road
Aldershot
Hants GU11 3HR
England

Ashgate Publishing Company
Old Post Road
Brookfield
Vermont 05036
USA

British Library Cataloguing in Publication Data

Economic Value and Ways of Life
   I. Eriksson, Ralf   II. Jäntti, Markus
   330.1

   ISBN 1 85972 076 5

Library of Congress Catalog Card Number: 95-76180

Reprinted 1997

Printed in Great Britain by Antony Rowe Ltd., Chippenham, Wiltshire

Contents

Acknowledgments

Lars Hertzberg is, in a sense, one of the editors of this volume. He brought together all the authors at seminars at the Department of Philosophy at Åbo Akademi University. The idea for this book originated in the research project "Ethics and the Economy" (1990-1993), which he led and which was funded by the Academy of Finland. He discussed the topics of most contributions with the individual authors and commented on their texts. But more important, he has created an atmosphere in which scholarly work can thrive and in which academics from different fields can get involved in the give and take of philosophical discussion. Lars chose to ask us to carry out the editorial work. We, in turn, choose to dedicate this book to him.

Most of the texts in this book were discussed in one form or another at seminars at the Department of Philosophy at Åbo Akademi University. The editors want especially to thank Göran Torrkulla, Nikolai Enckell, Olli Lagerspetz and Christian Burman for many valuable comments and constructive criticism. Most of the authors have also participated in these seminars and we would like to extend our thanks to them for not only contributing through their texts but also by helping us and each other see more clearly.

Christer Sundqvist provided valuable assistance in preparing the manuscript.

Finally, we would like to thank Georg Henrik von Wright for reading the entire manuscript and providing us with encouraging comments.

Production of this book

This book was produced using non-commercial software, i.e., software that is either in the public domain or under a so-called GNU-license (of the Free Software Foundation). This book was edited using Richard Stallman's GNU Emacs version 19, utilizing the AUCTeX system by Kresten Krab Thorup

and Per Abrahamsen. It was typeset using TEX, a computerized typesetting
system by Donald E. Knuth and LATEX, an extension of TEX originally written
by Leslie Lamport, with later enhancements by numerous contributors. The
bibliography was created using Oren Patashnik's BIBTEX program and the
index using the makeindex program. With the exception of the computer
hardware (a NeXTstation and a SparcStation ELC), the resources used to
create this book have been given by generous individuals to useful use. The
world of Public Domain and GNU-License software is to us evidence that not
everything that is valuable has a price.

Notes on contributors

Jan Otto Andersson is Reader in International Economics, Åbo Akademi University, Åbo, Finland

Ralf Eriksson is Research Associate in Economics, Åbo Akademi University, Åbo, Finland

Lars Hertzberg is Professor of Philosophy, Åbo Akademi University, Åbo, Finland

Markus Jäntti is Research Associate in Economics, Åbo Akademi University, Åbo, Finland

Tage Kurtén is Reader in Systematic Theology, Åbo Akademi University, Åbo, Finland

Jakob Meløe is Professor Emeritus of Philosophy, University of Tromsø

Hannes Nykänen is a Doctoral Candidate in Philosophy, Åbo Akademi University, Åbo, Finland

Juha Räikkä is Research Associate in Philosophy, University of Turku and Academy of Finland, Åbo, Finland

Vivan Storlund is a Doctoral Candidate in Law, University of Lund, Lund, Sweden

Elizabeth Wolgast is Professor in Philosophy, California State University, Hayward, U.S.A

Introduction

Ralf Eriksson and Markus Jäntti

Economics is the (social) science that purports to understand why human beings act in particular economic situations as they do, as well as to predict how they will act in some other situation. Often economics is about prices: why some commodities cost more than others and why the prices of certain commodities change. One of the great classical problems was the *value paradox*: why do some infinitely valuable goods, such as water have a price very much below that of some quite marginally useful goods, such as diamonds?

It would seem that questions of *value* and *valuation* should lie at the heart of economic analysis. However, as Mirowski (1989, 141) notes, one of the books that form the core of modern economic theory, Gerard Debreu's (1959) promisingly titled *Theory of Value* never discusses the problem of valuation.

This 'refining' of the conception of 'value' may be seen from different perspectives, for instance as a sign of the 'positivization' of economics, i.e. making a distinction between 'the positive' and 'the normative'. This in turn is a clear demarcation towards philosophy, i.e. it makes a difference between 'values', 'ethics' on one hand and 'economic science' on the other. Supplementing/alternating this view we may say that the modern definition of economic value is a manifestation of the division of labour and thus an example of the general tendency in modern society of specialization. Consequently, it may be claimed, as in other parts of society this is rational and signifies an increase in efficiency.

Although specialization certainly has its benefits – as every economist would hasten to underscore – it is not without drawbacks either. The advantages of bringing ethics back into economics have recently been emphasized by a host of writers. To keep this introduction within proper limits we only want to refer to Sen (1988) for a clear statement of the problem and to

1

Hausman and McPherson (1993) for a survey.

With this background in mind, it is perhaps fair to warn the reader: what follows will not be a clear-cut, systematic contribution to a new 'ethical economics' (whatever that may be) or a 'general theory of value', not to speak about some 'applied ethics' or 'professional ethics'. Towards the last-mentioned – we may note in passing – most, if not all of the present writers, are sceptical. To put it bluntly, most of us might argue along the following lines: The question of professional ethical codification seems to be based on the view that by superimposing 'ethical rules' upon, say, a firm, we get something that is called ethical and moral (and of course as a by-product, more efficient) behaviour out of it. We do not want to deny that such rules may be of practical importance, *if* they are followed. However, if such rules do not correspond to the moral sentiments of the community they are no more than lip-service and have very little indeed to do with what should properly be considered ethics.

Accordingly, this volume is an attempt to locate, circumscribe and/or 'wonder' – to paraphrase Nykänen (essay 8 below) – at the role(s) of economic values in society from different perspectives. A common feature in all the contributions in the approach to values seems to be the focus on the 'economizing' world-view, which – this sounds dangerously near a cliché – seems to have greatly permeated the 'modern way' of looking at life. However, this is not a feature to be attributed only to, e.g., Nobel laureate Gary Becker, but more important, we think, an unconscious feature of the world-view of 'modern western man'. A quite concrete example of this is Hertzberg's example of the modern way of looking at waste as an 'impoverished sense'(compared to the view of the native Americans of his example).

We do not want to claim that what is written below represents an amazingly new (turn of) perspective. Rather we would emphasize that this – discussing values – is a perennial theme which has been going on for a long, perhaps a very long time, indeed. As for the academic community, this discussion has perhaps as long a tradition as the community itself. For instance, in Aristotle's work values and virtues occupy a central place but we are inclined to believe Polanyi (1968), that he did not have much to say about what we here call 'economism'. This, we believe, is simply because the commercial way of life (i.e. the market economy) was but a small sphere of life in the Athens which Aristotle observed.

By the time of the height of the Schoolmen, we may say that the evolution of capitalism already had achieved such a spread that they obviously saw it necessary to devote relatively much more space to the conflict between commercial and spiritual values than Aristotle did. This impression is strengthened by looking at Schumpeter's *magnum opus*.[1] According to this the Schoolmen "repeated but qualified Aristotle's views on commerce and commercial gains" (Schumpeter 1955, 91). However, "they were the first to ask [...] the question why interest is actually paid" (Schumpeter 1955, 102).

However, to make a long story short, Adam Smith attempted to solve the conflict – at the ethical and theoretical level – between economic values, e.g. the rational pursuit of gain for oneself, which was considered a vice, or at best a necessary evil, and the moral virtues which were considered to be for the common good. We may say that although Aristotelian ethics was not useful for the solution of this conflict another part of his philosophy – natural law – proved to be so. With natural law philosophy – and not an insignificant stimulation from Bernard Mandeville – Smith was able to show[2] that self-interested behaviour could not be a damaging feature in man, but must be, through the working of the invisible hand – the market mechanism – beneficial for the whole society. Once the moral obstacle of the 'evil' of profit-seeking was removed, the stage for 'the free development' of economic value was set – in practice as well as in theory.

A recent discussion worth mentioning, to which the present essays are related, has taken place in economic anthropology.[3] We have already referred to Polanyi's anthropological analysis of Aristotle's writings. Polanyi's work was a main source of inspiration for a school within economic anthropology, the 'substantivists'. The substantivists emphasized that there are several ways to organize the livelihood of man. What we tend to call work, consumption, capital etc., were in ancient societies organized by the tribe or the state according to religious and other norms. What we call the market had but a limited and marginal role and was subordinated and sanctioned by principles that did not emanate from the market system.

Against this interpretation stood the 'formalists' who claimed that economic principles are universal, i.e., that concepts as scarcity, marginalist thinking etc. apply to human societies independently of time and place.

Perhaps it should be noted here that the question is not about whether a society could be shown to rest on principles of optimality in their use of resources. It can of course be true that the 'economy' as a life supporting system is optimal in some sense, (i.e., the use of resource should not exceed the productivity of the resource base). But this is another thing than to say that people behave like conscious individual maximizers. Or we could

---

[1]The expression 'evolution of capitalism' in this connection is Schumpeter's, who stresses the importance of the rise of capitalism in the period of Scholasticism (Schumpeter 1955, 78ff.).

[2]For references and further discussion, see Eriksson's essay.

[3]For a recent review see Lodewijks (1994).

say that it is not a question about whether modern (neoclassical) thinking could be applied to an ancient form of society. Of course we *could* apply, say, marginalist thinking to some behavior, e.g. the manufacturing of tools. The question is, however, whether the economic explanation gives a correct description of the terms in which man in that society himself reasons? From the fact that the result of some action may be optimal (which it may be in some sense, or not), it does not at all follow that the way in which the result was achieved in terms of chains of reasoning, motivating factors etc. follow modern economics textbooks.[4]

We are here perhaps at the abyss between *explanation* and *understanding* and we will not step further. However, we do not think that we have got it all wrong when we say that the present writers seem to be inclined to claim that the economic toolbox should be used with great care when looking at, e.g., historical communities and societies.

Now a natural question arising from this conclusion is how we should approach our own form of living. If the commercial values really have permeated life today, is not *homo oeconomicus* a convenient shorthand way of describing and analysing this?

We think that the present writers would agree that there is a proper sphere where this is the case. What is 'proper' cannot be decided once and for all here. But we may say that 'economizing' does not represent anything 'more fundamental' or 'basic' in human behaviour, but is but a(nother) cultural perspective. But as such it is definitely deficient and insufficient. For how can we criticize an (economic) culture from an economic perspective? Only in terms of optimality and efficiency.[5]

And this is a point where we could shake hands with traditional economics of the non-imperialist kind. If economics has become our values, then there is something wrong with the values, economics or both.

---

[4] A true 'formalist' would of course claim here that the economic analysis lays bare the 'real thing' and that the reasoning of a monk or a 'primitive' man, to the extent that it would proceed in terms really different from ours, would rest on an illusion.

[5] As a matter of fact this is exactly what sociobiology is about: to make cultural criticism a form of economics.

Overview of the chapters

Markus Jäntti addresses in chapter 1 ethical issues in debates on economic inequality. Distributive justice is often at the center of public and academic debate. Different sets of moral principles, such as classical utilitarianism, John Rawls's *justice as fairness* or egalitarianism, offer ways of deciding on how to judge in particular situations. When moral judgments on equity issues differ, we are often at a loss. We have little idea of how to decide when conflicts that emanate from different ethical theories arise, nor do we have much idea of how to understand such differences. They easily seem like matters of taste to us; in conflicts of taste, reason has little role.

The purpose of Jäntti's essay is to see if the understanding of such differences could be made more tractable. He suggests that the method of *wide reflective equilibrium* could be usefully employed to gain a better understanding of why and in what respects people differ when they arrive at opposite moral judgments regarding some distributional question. Jäntti argues that 'general' moral principles can lead to strongly counter-intuitive results, because they admit no role for either the way in which the social situation arose or for the consequences of different plans of action. If such considerations are deemed relevant, then some way of incorporating them into the decision procedure would seem desirable. For such an inclusion, the author argues, the method of reflective equilibrium offers a promising path. The author discusses the claims of Friedrich A. Hayek (that the concept of distributive justice is nonsense) and Arthur Okun (that the goal equity is in conflict with and should be balanced against the goal of efficiency) and interprets these using the method as a heuristic device.

Ralf Eriksson studies in essay 2 the rise of the market order and the 'economic mind' as illuminated by Friedrich A. Hayek's thoughts. The purpose is to interpret Hayek's thoughts about rules that produce (a certain) order ('a way of life'), within a functionalistic framework. Instead of taking self-interest as given, it is seen as a result of a historical development, as a result of a 'sequence of orders' (and rules). This means that the modern way of life with its values is seen as a product of cultural evolution. In Hayek's thought self-interested and calculating behaviour is anything but the self-evident feature it may seem to be today. It is *but a part* of man's moral heritage, a part of moral development – neutrally speaking (of which Hayek of course emphasizes the beneficial aspects). Instead of the viewing man in modern society as a realization of his 'inner nature', in some sense (as seems to be the presumptional background in much scientific work, public policy or popular debate) we could rather (bluntly) characterize Hayek's view as that of a realization of man's fate.

Tage Kurtén contrasts in essay 3 two central activities of modern life, *work* and *consumption*. As a point of departure, basing himself on interviews with Finnish writers and other work considering work ethics, Kurtén firstly discusses the view that consumption and 'consumerism' represent relative (and external) values, but work more fundamental, 'absolute' (internal) values.

However, not all absolute values have to be of a moral kind. Taking one's work for granted and then getting unemployed certainly is a situation where the basis of existence is felt to waver for most of us. But such an uncertainty may have many other grounds than moral ones, such as losing your earnings, losing your work-mates, social status etc. However, the case may also be that the person has 'internalized' values of honour etc. The meaning of such sets of values, as in 'protestant work ethics' is illuminated by Kurtén also from a religious perspective.

However, as has in this introduction repeatedly been pointed out, 'consumerism' seems to have acquired a life of its own, i.e. economistic values have acquired an absolute character (as must be the case also with much of work in the modern sense also, we suspect). Quoting the catholic philosopher and theologican J. F. Kavanaugh Kurtén notes that

> True moral conflicts arise, however, when, in our well-founded and sane recognition that things, production, consumption, technical reason, even competition, cannot and should not be ignored in the building of human life, we accept these values as ultimate. (Kurtén, this volume, 80)

Once the absoluteness of "the commodity form" or consumerist way of life is adopted (consciously or unconsciously), the human being can but be judged on these (economic) terms, i.e. as a commodity. It is against this background of this perceived emptiness of commercial values that Kurtén can maintain – in our opinion correctly[6] – that the positive valuation of work and the criticism of consumption should be understood.

That the present authors agree that values *may* and do change should be quite clear from what has already been said. But how do we evaluate these changes? How quickly do such changes occur? These questions are discussed by Juha Räikkä in essay 4 with reference to "contemporary Western values"

---

[6]However what we find difficult to understand is the high intrinsic status which seems to be inherent in industrial work. As a matter of fact one could claim that as with "Modern Times" (cf. Chaplin) man has lost his independence and dignity in many kinds of work, he seems to have substituted this loss with increased consumption, e.g. by showing off to other people. So consumerism *might* be seen as an effect rather than the cause of economizing values – reification.

during the last ten to fifteen years. It is often claimed that we live in a the midst of a value crisis, or that there is an *embarras de richesse* of values or that there are no longer any values in the West. Räikkä analyzes these claims and notes that in all cases this change in values is considered to be a bad thing. Against what background can this claim be based? We may judge values against the values of past, the values of the present, the values of the future and 'time-independent', eternal values. Of these Räikkä is most sympathetic towards judging values against (the coherence of) other contemporary values. An argument in favour of this view is that values that are typically (effectively?) referred to are accepted at the present time. For instance, criticism of slavery in 19th century America was justified by referring to another present value, that of individual freedom. Also, reference to present or future values are often but present values in disguise.

If we accept (some) current values as a standard of judging (other) current values we must also accept the view that not *all* current values can be bad.

But to say that not all our values can be bad is a claim that is separable from saying that our values have progressed or deteriorated. Räikkä discusses the claim that our values have progressed. This claim rests on the following two premises. Firstly, that our values have converged and, secondly, that a convergence of values indicates progress. Räikkä concludes that the convergence thesis is plausible, "if not unproblematic" (e.g., convergence may be merely formal). Concerning the second premise we may say that it is critically dependent on the time span we are studying. What we consider convergence today may well merely be a momentary trend in an otherwise divergent or perhaps random movement, considered from a future point of view.

A dialogue – of which this volume as a whole hopefully also is part of – between the economic and a non-economic, 'holistic', way of looking at life is carried out in Elizabeth Wolgast's essay 5. Wolgast compares two ways of looking at life: the more traditional anthropologic and the economic one. It should perhaps be emphasized that the economic view that Wolgast depicts here is not any form of unflinching economism.[7]

We could perhaps summarize Wolgast's discussion as a question: If members of a group of people do not understand what they are doing and how they are thinking in economic terms, can we interpret that in economic terms? A scientific-economic answer would be affirmative. For instance a 'primitive' society in which the members claim to be living, say, totally in accordance

---

[7]At the end of the essay, Wolgast discusses what could perhaps be called "Beckerian fundamentalism", i.e., the view that whatever institution or behavior one may observe, it is just a manifestation of the same fundamental human characteristics ('values'). However Wolgast dismisses this view as "parochial".

to the will of their forefathers is just seemingly doing so. Fundamentally, 'really', when we go behind their delusion we can show that they are following
economic principles.

Wolgast is inclined to answer the question negatively. She points out,
in our view correctly, that our tendency to separate different aspects of a
society – and think of this as natural and unequivocal – is nothing but a
cultural trait, a prejudice. This means that we do not see any more clearly
than others what they are doing, as is implied in the above 'fundamentalistic'
claim. The economic view does not represent something more fundamental,
scientific than a religious or a political view. It is just *one* way of looking at
life.

In his study of the uses of the word 'waste' (essay 6) we think that Lars
Hertzberg addresses the central theme of this volume, seen both as what
unifies the separate endeavors as well as a general (if perhaps not always
explicit) aim. This is about the 'givenness' of a view of life on the one hand
but on the other also about the possibility of (and we dare to add: the
necessity of trying to) deliberating on this. We think the following passage
summarizes this theme:

> [T]he economic perspective of life is not one that we are free either
> to retain or to discard like a pair of glasses. It would be an illusion
> to suppose that we could simply cease to be economics-minded
> without a radical concurrent change in our whole way of life. This
> does not mean, however, that we may not strive to become aware
> of the limitations of this perspective, of the ways in which it may
> distort matters or the things it may tend to hide from our sight.
> For even if we have a tendency to see things from an economic
> point of view, we are not incapable of regarding things in other
> ways as well. (Hertzberg, this volume, 104)

Hertzberg's own deliberating effort focuses mainly on the borderline between 'the market' and other institutions, such as legislation, and more interesting, what we may call moral convictions, sentiments or commitments.
What is considered economically possible or legitimate (what is considered
the 'economics sphere', or the 'market proper') varies, upon a closer look,
'right before our eyes', as in Hertzberg's holy water example. What is called
'business' in one (sub?)culture (such as a bank robbery) may be totally unthinkable in another (and to the degree a certain deed is thinkable it is also
disastrous for that culture).

The essay by Hertzberg considerably restricts the proposed universality of
what may be called 'the project of omnipotent economics' (of which the works
of Gary Becker provide a prominent example). It is also a useful reminder

to the otherwise oblivious economics professional about the restrictions on self-interest (moral, institutional) which Adam Smith talked about.

To summarize Jakob Meløe's essay 7 turns out to be at the same time a difficult and an easy task for the editors. The 'allegoric' nature on the one hand makes a conclusion both difficult if not impossible, but the shortness of the essay on the other hand makes a conclusion unnecessary. The reader is invited, of course, to enjoy the essay himself. In relating the essay to the main theme of this volume we must be content with the following conclusion. The limited role which is given to 'economy' in his allegory of life as haymaking (or perhaps haymaking as life) is perhaps the closest modern man can approach the traditional rural way of looking at the economy. Someone with, say, a working-class background from Liverpool would have given another allegory, perhaps a more economically imbued one with concepts like selling one's work-power, etc. And on Wall Street life *is* about making money and doing calculations. To make haymaking *the* story of life on Wall Street would probably be as misleading as making economic calculation *the* story of life in Northern Norway.

With this rather self-evident complementary addition we do not intend to say that the content and meaning of Meløe's story is exhausted. On the contrary, we think that Meløe's picture as such serves a powerful (some would perhaps say romantic) contrast between modern and 'rural' values concerning the good life.

At first sight Hannes Nykänen's essay 8 may seem to be a bit apart from the central theme of this volume. However, upon a closer look it is in a sense more directly to the point. While many of the other chapters – as already noted – seem to be fully occupied circumscribing the problem, in Nykänen's chapter the focus is on one 'concrete' phenomenon of modern life, i.e. modern (serious) music.

Nykänen contrasts two attitudes towards life: let us here abbreviate them as "wonder" and "control". It is perhaps not too wrong to say that wonder is the pre-modern attitude, while control is the modern one that has grown with scientific technology. The former is characterized by respect and humility for Nature while the latter is characterized by a manipulative and an instrumental interest. At the political level the former concepts are associated with obligation, while while the latter are associated with rights (to demand something).

The attitude of control or the technological understanding of being is then shown by Nykänen to have extended to all walks of life – even contemporary music: "The essence of contemporary music is such that it is incompatible with any response connected with wonder" (Nykänen, this volume, 135). Rather than being struck by wonder our "response is in some sense about 'complexity'" (ibid. 136). Thus, we may say, the sacredness of music is lost and our relation to music has became an external one. Nykänen shows, for instance, that John Cage's chance-music is not, as is often claimed, a rejection of calculation in music. Rather it may be seen as an extreme form of calculative thinking, i.e., as the introduction of probability calculations into composing. Also minimalistic music, which is often thought to be spontaneous and simple, is shown to require extreme control, e.g., in the repetition of a theme.

Vivan Storlund's essay 9 is a critique of contemporary law and the *Rechtsstaat* as construed according to the world view of classical economics. Storlund, basing herself on Galbraith and Huberman emphasizes that the formulation of law has not been able to follow up the social change that has occurred during the last centuries. Besides this, the analysis of law is permeated by the economic view in another way. The deductive reasoning applied to legal decision-making is a deficient explanation. The deductive explanation does not account for "our ability to distinguish between correct and incorrect decisions". Instead, "[j]udicial decisions, just like the judgements of lawyers, are based on reasons, and the reasons that both have been taught to consider relevant are of the same kind" (Hertzberg 1981, quoted by Storlund, this volume, 143 and 144). The individualist-atomist picture of society has continued to have a hold on administrators and lawyers of today. Transnational corporations and international capital are equalized with physical persons and are supposed to represent autonomous and morally responsible persons. In reality, as Wolgast (1992) has shown, in "artificial persons" "institutional practices can have priority over moral claims" (Storlund, this volume 151). To remedy this lack of responsibility, Storlund proposes a theoretical scheme built on theories of social justice of John Rawls, David Miller and Wojciech Sadurski.

That the proposed "value freedom" of so-called mainstream economics is a value in itself has been noted several times in this introduction. This has (at least) two implications. Firstly, 'value freedom' – even if such a thing could exist in some hermetic, ideal world – cannot of course be an absolute end in itself. Secondly, the 'practical' welfare economics is still forced to use tools that are all but value free, such as utilitarian calculus.

Jan Otto Andersson proposes in essay 10 to get rid of this double standard of morality (or delusion) and instead make the ideals conscious and visible. The ideals or values which Andersson proposes are "real freedom", "democratic community" and "sustainable development".

Real freedom encompasses perhaps one of the most beautiful thoughts of the liberal tradition: man's self-realization and and self-understanding, seen from the positive view of freedom and capability to do something. Paradox-ical as it may seem to someone with an atomistic view of the world, this 'individualization' can only take place within a community. Individual and individualistic values, of course, are a result of a 'cultural climate' and a socialization process. Once this is noted, it is evident that human freedom must be located in the 'community space' and thus be submitted to the decisions of the democratic community. But even if the community puts restraints on one individual's desires to balance them against those of other individuals', it may be that the desires of the whole community intrude on spheres of life which are not covered by the ideals of liberty and democracy. These spheres are those of future generations and (living) nature. This is why the ideal of sustainable development is needed in parallel with the two others. Perhaps one could say in a suitably idealistic spirit that the role of the democratic community is to 'discuss' the 'proper emphasis' on each of these values. As a result of this discussion the individual would be made aware of the restrictions to his desires and his view of his capabilities would reflect 'the true' restrictions put by (a chosen) way of sustainable development.

There are of course numerous ways in which these essays are interconnected, which we do not have room to explicate here. We hope that the patient reader will find the discovery and understanding of these worth while.

1 Economic inequality and reflective equilibria

Markus Jäntti

Introduction

> It is generally agreed that, other things being equal, a considerable reduction in inequality of incomes would be desirable.

(Dalton 1920, 348)

> The contrasts among American families in living standards and in material wealth reflect a system of rewards and penalties that is intended to encourage effort and channel it into socially productive activity. To the extent that the system succeeds, it generates an efficient economy. But that pursuit of efficiency necessarily creates inequalities. And hence society faces a tradeoff between equality and efficiency.

(Okun 1975, 1)

The above quotations summarize what I take to be both popular and academic beliefs about income inequality in modern industrialized societies. That more equality as such would be a good thing, if nothing else had to change to achieve this (Dalton). But, more equality will reduce the perceived or real incentives and thus there will be less growth. "Other things" will not be equal, hence we should live with at least some of the inequality the market generates (Okun).

Matters of distributive justice are often at the center of public and academic debate. Many different sets of moral principles, such as classical utilitarianism, *justice as fairness* or egalitarianism, offer ways of deciding on how to judge in particular situations. When implications differ, we are often at a loss. We have little idea of how to decide when conflicts that emanate from different ethical convictions arise, nor do we have much idea of how to understand such differences. They easily seem like matters of taste to us; in conflicts of taste, reason has little role.

The purpose of this chapter is to see if the understanding of such differences could be made more tractable. Specifically, I suggest that the method of *wide reflective equilibrium* (WRE) could be usefully employed to gain a better understanding of why and in what respects people differ when they arrive at opposite moral judgements regarding some distributional question.

How do we arrive at particular moral judgements? Moral theories, as any theories, are subject to some process of formation and justification. We clearly do hold moral views and make moral judgements. How we arrive at and justify these is of central interest in this chapter.

I use the method of WRE to try to understand (some of) the reasons why people disagree on claims of economic equality. In particular, I attempt to show that differences in moral judgements and in moral principles can often be traced back to theories of how the economy works, of justice, moral actions and so on. Such an understanding might allow us to discriminate among competing conceptions of distributive justice; however, I shall not argue so here. I shall merely be concerned with showing what types of disagreement conceal themselves behind the opposite judgements on inequality.

I do so by presenting an example of a social situation of increased economic inequality. I show that the three moral principles presented above can lead to strongly counter-intuitive results, because they admit no role for either the way in which the social situation arose or for the consequences of different plans of action. If such considerations are deemed relevant (which, I argue, is intuitively acceptable), then some way of incorporating them into the decision procedure would seem desirable. For such an inclusion, I argue that the method of reflective equilibrium offers a promising path.

More importantly, however, I attempt to understand how widely differing claims regarding the proper role of distributive justice can be made intelligible by using reflective equilibria as a heuristic device. I show that the claims of both F.A. Hayek (that the concept of distributive justice is nonsense) and Arthur Okun (that the goal equity is in conflict with and should be balanced with the goal of efficiency) can be interpreted using this device, and how the claims can be traced back to the background social and economic theories the writers hold.

In what follows, I use the concepts of distributive justice and economic equity interchangeably, not because they are exactly identical, but because they are sufficiently similar for the purposes of this chapter. I also use economic equality to mean a state where economic equity has been realised, although sometimes it will also indicate a situation where an egalitarian distribution has taken place.

I argue that meaningful statements regarding economic inequality can only be made in a specific context. Thus, while not exactly an empirical question, the moral status of inequality-statements is at the very least related to the empirical circumstances in which they are posed. It makes little sense to separate 'technical' from 'moral' aspects (or rather to presuppose either). The moral status of statements regarding inequality depends on all specifications, means and mechanisms of the context, moral and technical alike.

Theories of distributive justice

Charles Taylor (1985) contrasts what he calls atomistic views of society and distributive justice with views which explicitly acknowledge society as the locus in which man realizes what he deems good. Classical utilitarianism is an example of atomistic views, as is, in some sense, Rawls's justice as fairness. Atomistic doctrines typically do not make reference to the particular situation in which they are to be applied, but are universal or mechanical in formulation. Concepts of distributive justice that take man in society as their starting point will typically have to resort to desert and merit, among other things, in order to arrive at judgements regarding justness.

The three most common contenders for a universal ethical theory of distribution would seem to be utilitarianism, *justice as fairness* and egalitarianism. Justice as fairness rests on two principles. John Rawls argues that in an original position where people would be behind a *veil of ignorance*, they should rationally agree upon two (hierarchically ordered) principles of justice and that these principles can be considered fair.[1] These are that:

1. Each citizen has an equal right to the most extensive scheme of equal basic liberties compatible with a similar scheme of liberties for all.

2. Social and economic inequalities are to satisfy two conditions: they must be (a) to the greatest benefit of the least advantaged members of society; and (b) attached to offices

---

[1]The veil of ignorance refers to the thought experiment Rawls makes which is understood as a situation where a person knows the personal characteristics of all the members of society but is ignorant as to who he or she is (or will be) in society (Rawls 1971, 136).

and positions open to all under conditions of fair equality of
opportunity. (Rawls 1982, 161–162)

The two principles would, according to Rawls, be the rational choice of
any person behind the veil of ignorance. However, principle 2.a, the *maximin-*
principle, does not really provide us with a method of deciding between
different distributions, other than in a very limited sense. More specifically,
it fails to meet our intuitions regarding inequalities, since only the income of
the least well-off are focused on.

For the purposes of the present chapter, I treat egalitarianism as the
principle that the social state where incomes are equal should be chosen.[2]

Classical utilitarianism requires that one choose the social state which
maximizes the sum of individual utilities (which, if the number of individuals is constant, is equivalent to maximizing the arithmetic average of utility).
Utilitarianism has acquired a reputation for egalitarianism, as several authors
have noted.[3] This reputation is due to the coincidence of two very special and
logically independent assumptions. Firstly, there is the definition of utilitarianism, namely, that the social state (distribution) which, for a given total
income, maximizes the sum of individual utilities should be chosen.[4] Secondly, it is assumed that all individuals have identical utility functions that
are concave in income. Only then will the egalitarian distribution maximize
social welfare. There are very few situations where everybody is actually assumed to possess the same utility function.[5] Once the assumption of identical
utility functions is relaxed, there is little egalitarianism left in utilitarianism.
Indeed, utilitarianism has very little at all to say on distributions unless all
utility functions are known, or, alternatively, imposed by the decision-maker.

Consider the following example. Imagine a small community, an island,
perhaps. There are (only) two companies in the community, both manufacturing (different) export goods. One, company *A*, has been successful in
business, being very profitable and paying high wages to its workers. The
other, company *B*, has been far less successful and pays lower wages than *A*.
Suppose also that employees remain with the firm they start with (this is to
rule out the possibility of a movement of workers across firms).

Assume that a change in the economic environment occurs, say, that the
price of company *B*'s product falls substantially. Profits are already pressed

---

[2]See Baker (1992), for a more elaborate formulation.
[3]See, e.g., Sen (1973) or Stiglitz (1982).
[4]Note also, the all utilities are assumed to have equal weights.
[5]Peculiarly, although interpersonal comparisons of utility have long been banished from
economics, in much empirical work researchers use models of representative consumers
and seldom consider the consequences of heterogeneous preferences. In effect, in much
empirical work, people do have interpersonally comparable utilities.

to the limit; the only way for company *B* to continue its activity is by cutting the wages it pays to its workers. The employees agree, with the result that the distribution of income is substantially more unequal than prior to the adverse change.

How should we judge the new distribution of income? If we think the new situation is in some sense bad, how should we respond? In what way does our required response vary with our role in (this) society? If equality of income were the only goal, then (vulgar) egalitarians should, for instance, require that employees of company *A* throw into the sea income in excess of what those working for *B* earn. Or, (less absurdly) they could require that employees in *A* and *B* share their earnings so that incomes are equated.

We could, on the other hand, approach this from the point of view of those involved. Employees of company *A* have clearly done nothing wrong. They have gone about their business quite as usual. Also, employees in company *B* have done nothing wrong. By no fault of theirs, prices on the products they manufacture just dropped, as did their earnings. There are no guilty parties to extract compensation from (I am abstracting from the possibility of class-conflict between capitalists and workers).

Indeed, why should we worry about the resulting distribution? No-one has committed a crime, some outside (exogeneous) influence just happened to affect relative prices; end of story. If re-training of workers is possible, it is likely some workers from *B* would migrate to *A*. That, however, is not our concern here.

I think there are two main ways in which moral judgements and moral action enters a story like this. First, what consequences will the new distribution have on people? Will *B*'s employees or their dependents suffer from unmet needs after the pay cuts? Will they go hungry, badly clothed, unsheltered? Will society become less safe or stable as a result of increasing gaps in living standards? Will the children of *B*'s workers have less opportunities in life (e.g. of education) because of these changes? In short, what will the effects on the people concerned, both *B*'s workers and their families, and the rest of society be of the change? Second, assume that there was and is some form of government in our society, financing its activities by taxes on labour income. How should government react? Should it change its tax and transfer schedule? These are not unrelated questions. Rather, they are ways of looking at what kind of moral claims will be made and what moral duties recognized, which moral claims will be thought to be justified and in what manner these moral claims will be honoured. These questions relate to the question: what types and which consequences of economic inequality are matters of public concern?

Arriving at moral judgements

Let us return to the example of two companies and government taxes. Given that there is a government with power to tax and re-distribute, (i) both egalitarians and Rawlsians will tax and transfer until post-tax and -transfer distributions are equal and that (ii) if the assumption is accepted that utility (or welfare) functions of all citizens are identical and strictly concave in income, the classical utilitarian will also equalize incomes. (If we are unwilling to assume identical utility functions, classical utilitarianism is a non-starter as a decision procedure).

But under what circumstances would it be just to equalize incomes? For instance, assume that workers are at an early age assigned randomly to each industry. It could be argued that because of this, inequalities of income are unjustified, for instance, because *ex ante* and *ex post* incomes are so different; justice calls for an equalization of these. Or, assume that work in *A* is more physically exhausting than in *B*, people are fully aware of this at the point at which they choose their employment, so that the resulting distribution of employees is according to their preference for 'hard' vs. 'easy' work. Or, assume that the effect of the discrepancy in incomes will be that children of the low-income group will face far fewer economic opportunities (say to choose to be in *A* or in *B*) than those in the high-income group.

We could go on inventing examples of different circumstances or consequences of the increased inequality of incomes in which we may or may not feel that an equalization of incomes would be just. What I want to achieve with this example is to point at two things. In making judgements about the appropriate scheme for redistribution, we simply cannot ignore the issues of (i) how the people involved came to be in their present situation and (ii) what consequences different courses of action will have. The application of a principle which does not account for or assign any role to merit, desert or consequences, as egalitarianism, classical utilitarianism or *justice as fairness* do, does not mesh well with our moral intuitions regarding what is equitable. As Le Grand (1991, 186) remarks, we are here looking for a way of making moral judgements which commands consensus on what is meant by equity. I think that an accepted definition would grant some role to merit, desert and/or consequences.

Justifying moral theories

If we do not have a ready-made answer to issues about inequality, how should we go about deciding on what the morally justified course of action in some specific question is? This leads us into the area of theory justification in moral philosophy. When a person is confronted with an ethical problem, one way to proceed is to apply some ethical principle and see whether this allows him to choose between the alternative solutions. For instance, confronted with the problem of choosing a tax/transfer schedule above, if we are classical utilitarians and assume identical utility functions, application of this principle leads us to equalize incomes. Application of justice as fairness also leads to this outcome.[6]

The problem with the slavish application of such 'complete' principles is that they leave no room for moral intuitions. We might have reasons not to completely equalize the distribution, reasons that are also based on moral reasoning (e.g., on desert). Neither do these principles assign any role to other, possibly non-moral considerations, such as those of efficiency or incentives. We can have quite adequate reasons to include such factors in our judgements on particular occasions. A satisfactory account of how we arrive at decisions should explicitly allow for such a possibility. Moral principles are like rules; we resort to these when making judgements in particular situations. We also use our intuitions: principles can rarely be complete.

Assume that the proponents of egalitarian tax/transfer schedules above show how, by appeal to Rawls's justice as fairness, such a scheme is equitable. This will almost certainly be against the opponents moral intuitions ('desert should be taken into account when making decisions'), but the moral principle applied takes no notice of this. Then the discussion will most likely move to a debate on the adequacy of justice of fairness: whether or not it is a good moral principle, would rational agents really arrive at those (and no other) principles. Indeed, the exclusion of moral intuitions from the sphere of relevant material to base decisions on leads to an obfuscating of the whole issue. From the question of what would be a good tax schedule the discussion moves on to the choice of moral principles, rather than to the consequences of actions for the people involved in terms of the goods of that particular society.

A method for justifying moral theories put forward by John Rawls is that of *reflective equilibrium*. A wide reflective equilibrium (WRE) can best be understood as an ordered triple of (a) a set of considered moral judgements, (b) a set of moral principles and (c) a set of relevant background theories, all three of which are internally consistent. The background theories in (c) should be such that the moral principles in (b) are more acceptable than some other set of moral principles, independently of the grounds for accepting (a)

---

[6]Note that I am using a very crude version of utilitarianism. See Sen and Williams (1982) for sophisticated versions.

as being in accordance with (b) (Daniels 1979). Assume that a moral agent engages in an argument on some particular moral judgement, say regarding economic inequality and that it is pointed out to him that some relevant background theory he relied on was erroneous. Thus, to attain a new WRE he should adjust his background theories, moral principles and/or considered judgements, perhaps moving back and forth, until a new equilibrium is reached.

The method of WRE can perhaps be thought of as an idealization of the end-result of a process by which a person forms his or her moral views (or theory). The main difference between WRE and narrow reflective equilibrium (NRE) is that in the latter, there is no appeal to the background theories (c). There are several interpretations of WRE. We can think of it as a description of how one person arrives at a consistent set of moral beliefs. We can also think of it as a way of arriving at true moral beliefs. Further, we can think of WRE as a way for groups of people to arrive at (the same) moral beliefs or finding moral truth. In this chapter I shall only use the first of these interpretations, i.e., that WRE is a way to understand the moral beliefs one individual holds.

An example of WRE could be constructed from the following. Assume you read in a newspaper that a young girl whose single mother receives welfare has saved some money to go to college (a story much like this appeared in the *New York Times* in the spring of 1992). Because of the means-test associated with welfare, when it is found that there are more savings in the household than the rules admit, the family is ordered to pay back some welfare received. These in turn have to be taken out of the daughter's savings and her plans to go to college fail. Assume that your initial moral judgement (a) is that it is wrong that the girl, who has worked after school and been very industrious, making plans in order to change her life rather than indulging in wasteful consumerism,, should lose her chances to go to college. On the other hand, you may have the moral principle (b) that people should primarily support themselves, and society should pay only for those who are not able to secure a living; the means-test follows as a corollary. There would then appear to be a gap between the initial considered judgement and the moral principle.

To attain NRE, we would merely adjust either, or both, our judgements and our principles. For WRE, we would resort also to appropriate background theories. Appropriate background theories would be some economic theory of labour supply, intergenerational correlation of socio-economic factors, socialization, moral hazard, human capital theories (stating that increased education is likely to increase earnings) and so on. A whole host of theoretical considerations, some consistent and some inconsistent with both our moral intuitions and our moral principles can be brought to bear on the problem. Adjusting both our principles and moral judgements, perhaps also the background theories, we may reach a new WRE.[7]

Rawls uses the method of WRE to derive his two principles of justice as fairness.[8] Critics point out serious deficiencies in the method of WRE. Firstly, WRE gives no guidance on how to select better moral principles, where better is understood as something other than 'more coherent'. Secondly, we have no guidance as to whether in WRE we are closer to moral truth than when we started out. Thirdly, although one person may attain a WRE, and other people may also attain it, there is no guarantee that they will converge at a common WRE (inter- vs. intra-personal WRE). Fourth, there is no guidance in the method as to from which end we should start revising our sets of beliefs. Should we rid ourselves of our current moral principles, adjust our beliefs or shop around for more appropriate background theories? Fifth, what view of moral truth the proponents of WRE subscribe to is left open. In effect, claim the critics, the method of WRE does not deliver what it promises: a way of getting closer to moral truth.

The method of WRE might not be a good description of how a single person or a group of people (society) *actually* arrives at moral beliefs, it might not be a good prescription of how single persons or groups *should* arrive at moral beliefs (although I am not arguing it isn't). Again, for the purposes of this chapter, these criticisms are not crucial. I am using the method to better understand moral disputes and to trace differences in RE to their origins. I also take it that the coherence requirement, so central to the idea of WRE, is not disputed; that, in effect, this is seen as an elementary requirement of any moral system. But it can be a useful tool for understanding why and how people differ in their moral assessments of similar situations.

Classes of judgements

Amartya Sen (1967) has provided some useful distinctions regarding different uses of prescriptive judgements. Some judgements are purely prescriptive, such as: "Let us abolish capital punishment". This is a pure imperative.

---

[7]An important criticism of WRE is that there is no guidance as to how adjustments are to be made. See Raz (1982).

[8]Rawls's use of the method has since been both defended, elaborated and criticized. See Daniels (1979) or Nielsen (1982) for elaborations and defenses, and Raz (1982) for criticism. The criticisms center around the claims that WRE would provide us with approximations of moral truth. For the purposes of this chapter, we need not concern us with the epistemic status of moral beliefs arrived at using WRE.

Some also have a descriptive component. These Sen calls evaluative: e.g., "Capital punishment is barbarous". Capital punishment is bad, because it has some of the descriptive features that are normally associated with that which is barbarous.

Moral judgements can also be partitioned according to what the judgement implies. Sen calls a *compulsive* moral judgement one in which a preference of X before Y implies that X should always be chosen. A non-compulsive judgement is one which involves an imperative, but not an unqualified one. For instance, one might say, "X is nicer than Y, but let's choose Y, just to keep up with fashion". There is a commendation to choose X over Y, but there are other, overriding reasons to choose Y. In such a case, it seems reasonable that the burden of proof is on alternative Y, i.e., unless good reasons are given in favor of Y, X is (should be) chosen. But to say: "X is nicer than Y. They are just the same otherwise. Let me not choose X." is unintelligible.

Value judgements can also be partitioned into basic and non-basic judgements. Sen (1967) calls a value judgement basic to a person if no revision of the factual assumptions will make the person revise the judgement. If factual assumptions change and this induces the person to revise his judgement, then the factual judgement can be called non-basic. For instance, a person might say that "A decrease in the proportion of poor people would be desirable". We could then inquire if this judgement would hold under all circumstances, e.g., if the reduction were to be obtained by further impoverishing a majority of the poor in order to lift out of poverty a small minority. If the person were to revise the judgement, we could call it non-basic. If, on the other hand, a person will not under any circumstances revise his conviction that killing a person is wrong, this judgement can be called basic to his value-system.

Usually, as Sen (1973) remarks, statements regarding economic equality are evaluative non-compulsive moral judgements. It would, indeed, be strange to say: "X entails less inequality than Y. They are just the same otherwise. Therefore, let us choose Y." If less equality is not chosen over more, there is a need to explain why. Thus, whether or not the alternative involving less equality is the justified choice depends on the circumstances, i.e., on more or less factual considerations. Thus, the statement: "X entails less inequality than Y. However, X involves a loss in total income compared with Y. Therefore, let us choose Y." is a logical statement. Note, however, that the burden of proof would in this case be placed on those who say that X would involve a loss in total income.

Equity and equality

It is sometimes implicitly (and at times explicitly) assumed that an equal distribution of resources would be equitable.[9] But to thus identify equity with equality is a mistake. It is one thing to say in some particular situation that more equality would lead to a more equitable distribution, and quite another to say that an equal distribution is desirable. Although we might, of course, under some particular set of circumstances hold both views, subscribing to the first but not to the second is not, in general, a contradictory position.

There are many well-known reasons why an equal distribution of resources could be argued to be inequitable. Examples of such are compensating differentials, i.e., the idea that people doing dirtier, heavier or more unpleasant work can be thought to deserve more pay. The disabled or sick have special needs that require more resources to be met.[10]

A set of problems with identifying equality of income with an equitable distribution of resources, that is often labelled 'practical', relates to differences in 'other equity-relevant characteristics', needs, for short.[11] The problem is, basically, the following. Are two families, A and B equally well-off with $ 10 000 a year, although A consists of a married childless couple and B consists of a married couple with five children? The common-sense answer is 'hardly'. But, what distribution of income would leave the two families equally well-off?[12] This is seldom treated as a difficult philosophical problem. Rather, it is solved by resorting to one of a few standard procedures for finding the equivalent distribution.[13] The logical form of the problem, however, is little different from the problems involving other special needs, or those regarding just compensation.

In empirical work on income inequality it is commonplace to distinguish between vertical and horizontal inequality. The former is usually identified with income inequality and the latter most often with the extent to which in-

---

[9]This is the case when inequality is measured using normative measures, which define the ideal distribution as the equal one, see e.g. Nygård and Sandström (1981).

[10]See, among others, Baker (1992) and the commentators, especially Barry.

[11]See Jenkins and Lambert (1992).

[12]For simplicity, I am abstracting from a whole host of serious problems. First, the family is hardly the unit where well-being is located, rather it is an individual experience (in which the family is very important, though). Second, if we can agree upon an equitable distribution between families, there remains the difficult question of what would represent an equitable distribution within the family, and, if and how it would be achieved. Thirdly, it is not self-evident that equal well-being is what equity requires (e.g., because of compensating differentials).

[13]For alternative methods, see Atkinson and Bourguignon (1987), Atkinson (1992), or Jenkins and Lambert (1992).

dividuals change places in the income distribution (so-called rank-reversals). Both of these phenomena are taken to represent inequities (Le Grand 1987). The usual definition of vertical and horizontal equity is that unequals should be treated unequally and equals should be treated equally. These problems are seldom treated as 'deep' philosophical problems, they are usually treated as problems of method. However, the answers to these problems depend on our considered moral judgements and are thus part of the ethical problem of how to make judgements regarding issues of distributive justice or economic equity.

Julian Le Grand (1991) argues that the most defensible conception of equity is that a distribution of resources is equitable if all individuals have equal choices. Thus, inequalities that are beyond an individual's control are inequitable, whereas those arising from different choices starting from similar possibilities are deemed equitable. This definition has the advantage of encompassing many notions that command some support, such as equality of opportunity, horizontal and vertical equity (equal treatment of equals and different treatment of unequals), or, for that matter, maximizing the position of the least well-off. Employment of this conception of equity might also serve to transform value debates on economic inequality to factual disagreements on whether or not in fact in some particular case choice sets were equal or not (it is unclear if this constitutes an improvement or not).

The equity-efficiency trade-off

Efficiency, i.e., the best use of scarce resources, is in conflict with an equal distribution of resources. But, equity is also valued, therefore we must find an optimal mix of efficiency and equitable distributions. This, in a nut-shell, is Arthur Okun (1975) "Big Trade-Off". Okun suggests a decision procedure to facilitate the finding of the optimal mix, the "Leaky-Bucket" experiment. This amounts to deciding how large a loss in production (efficiency) the decision-maker is prepared to accept in order to increase equality. Thus we have a set of background theories (c), a moral principle (b) which includes a mechanism for arriving at moral judgements (a) regarding the appropriate or optimal degree of equality in particular situations.

Okun's background theories (c) imply that efficiency and equity are in conflict, his set of moral principles (b) have it that both efficiency and equity are good, and decisions on the proportion in which the two blend should be made using a specific decision-making procedure, the leaky-bucket experiment, giving the judgements (a) in particular cases.

Okun's background theories include a special view of efficiency ("process efficiency") and a theory of production, which specifies the way in which the pursuit of equality produces inefficiencies. Okun's concept of efficiency is not tied to common definitions, such as Pareto-efficiency. Rather, it is process-oriented; to elicit effort, there need to exist observable levels of living higher than those that would otherwise be obtained. That effort in turn generates growth. When incomes are equalized, that growth-generating effort fails to be brought out, and, growth is less than it would have been.[14] The other way in which more equality produces less efficient outcomes is through the costs of redistributing.

Okun values both equality and efficiency (more material goods). Indeed, could he so choose, *ceteris paribus*, he would choose complete equality; issues of merit or compensating differentials do not appeal to him (p. 47). Okun's decision procedure, the leaky-bucket test is a thought experiment which helps him decide on a balance between efficiency and equity (p. 91). In the absence of equalizing transfers, there would be no leak (inefficiency) in the economy. But with existing inequalities, some leakage is acceptable if it is associated with equalizing effects. The amount of tolerable leakage is a function of the size of the disparities, but subject to the decision-maker to establish. The leakages consist of administrative costs, reduced work effort, reduced saving and investment, as well as "socioeconomic leakages" (p. 96) associated with taxation and redistribution. The leaky-bucket experiment appears to reduce the trade-off to a simple choice situation. By clearing the factual problems, i.e., the extent of leakage associated with a given redistribution of income, we can reveal our ethical preference in the form of a chosen threshold level of exchange, which lies somewhere between 0 and 100 per cent.

The more equality you wish to attain, the more you lose in efficiency. There are no market failures, asymmetric information and such, the type of short-comings of a market economy which for many economists provide justification for intervention (to promote efficiency, not to hinder it).[15] Introducing such elements into the background theories might force Okun to seek a new WRE, since his original judgements and principles, arrived at using the leaky-bucket experiment, would no longer be consistent with the underlying social theory.[16]

If the background theories have to be modified, e.g. if there are situations in which efficiency and equity are not in conflict, or where one type of

---

[14]This is different from the usual definition of efficiency found in economic theory, according to which an allocation is efficient if no-ones lot can be improved unless someone else's is worsened (Pareto-efficiency).

[15]See Barr (1992) for a review of the economic role of the welfare state.

[16]This perhaps shows the importance of WRE over NRE, where factual and theoretical considerations had no immediate role.

efficiency (e.g. Okun's process efficiency) is and some other type of efficiency (e.g. allocative efficiency) is not in conflict with equality, the triple would cease to be in WRE. For example, the presence of unemployment insurance can have the effect of promoting efficiency by enabling an unemployed person to wait for a job for which he has been trained (increasing, in a sense, the efficient allocation of education) but increasing inefficiency because one person has an incentive to remain outside the active labour force (he could be flipping hamburgers instead). On one hand, the existence of an equalizing transfer produces both an efficient and a more equal outcome (measured in income). On the other hand, it can be claimed to produce an inefficient outcome. The argument that is adopted depends on what type of efficiency you favour.

Hayek on distributive justice

Friedrich Hayek (1982b) provides a forceful critique not only of the ethical position regarding the desirability of equality over inequality, but of the whole concept of social or distributive justice.[17] Justice, as Hayek treats it, is only an attribute of the actions of individuals, not a property of self-ordering processes as he claims a free market to be. He makes no secret of his view that the whole concept of social justice is misconceived. He thinks it only a sign of the primitive state of our thinking that such ideas are aired at all. Only in special organizations, such as an army, do such concepts make sense, because they are not self-ordering. The social organization in such systems is non-spontaneous and hierarchical and therefore the logic of individual action is extended to the social organization. Justice considerations can not be applied to spontaneous processes, such as the market process.

It is, of course, questionable whether one may call Hayek's refutation of the concept of distributive justice a moral judgement in the sense I have been using the term. However, treating it as a moral judgement, based on the principle that effectively states the same, we can delve into Hayek's background theories to understand the reasons for this refutation. Hayek has theories of the person, a theory of economic processes, of knowledge, and indeed, of morality, which are in many respects radically different from any we have considered so far. This is not the place to review Hayek's social theory, but against that background his refutation of distributive justice makes sense. Hayek's moral views are coherent with his theory of economic and social activity. Because the results of the impersonal, self-ordering economic process

---

[17]I am using Hayek's terms here.

cannot be attributed to any individuals' actions, the results cannot be judged just or unjust; to so judge the results would be a category mistake. Justice is an attribute of human conduct, not a property of social states.

Interpreted as a WRE, Hayek's background theories (c) include a theory of the economy which gives, among other things, that left to itself, i.e., free from intervention, the market process brings the greatest possible material rewards to people in society. It does this by coordinating the actions of a large number of individuals in such a way that the resulting distribution of resources and goods is nobody's design, but has come about in an impersonal manner. His moral principles (b) include only such principles that regulate the justness of individuals' actions. Justice considerations are not appropriate when judging the result of a spontaneous order, such as the market process. Thus (a) in no situations can one decide that some distribution should be made more equitable.

But if the market process is not functioning properly, there might be some scope for what Hayek calls social justice claims. On the other hand, the claims of people who are unable to provide for themselves would probably be felt to be justified. Hayek does not under all circumstances disregard the concept of social justice; it is only under the idealized market rule that he does so, and even then he leaves room for some considerations which at least seem like those of social justice.

Le Grand (1991, 185) notes that Hayek would admit the possibility of distributional judgements when applied to non-spontaneous processes. Then, since in actual economies processes are not spontaneous, Le Grand concludes that Hayek would admit that social justice considerations are meaningful when applied to real world situations. This modification to Hayek's scheme is an adjustment of the background theories (c) in WRE. This conclusion stands or falls with Hayek's view of real world economic processes (although Le Grand bases his conclusion on *his own* observation that modern Western economies can hardly be called spontaneous (Le Grand 1991, 185). Hayek writes:

> The prevalent demand of material equality is probably often based on the belief that the existing inequalities are the effect of somebody's decision – a belief which would be wholly mistaken in a genuine market order and *has still very limited validity in the highly interventionist 'mixed' economy existing in most countries today.* This now prevalent form of economic order has in fact attained its character largely as a result of governmental measures aiming at what was thought to be required by 'social justice'. (p. 81, italics added)

Justice considerations can be applied to results of human decision. The problem of whether or not Hayek would condemn equity considerations as nonsense becomes on this view a question of *how limited* the validity of the belief – that inequities are the effect of deliberate decisions – is. In his criticism of the concept of social justice, Hayek focuses on the notion of just remuneration for work. But in reality, there are other sources of inequality than those of the market. Also, there are taxation and transfers. (This is basically Le Grand's point.) All of these (or at least taxes and transfers) are non-spontaneous. Would Hayek admit that social justice does have meaning in such issues (pp. 77-79)? Hayek is not quite clear when he discusses the difference between the role of justice-considerations in a spontaneous order and in existing mixed economic orders. Most claims on inequities do not rest on somebody deliberately being or acting in a manner which is inequitable, an impression Hayek's discussion conveys. However, decisions by individuals or groups of individuals certainly *affect* the distribution of material resources – at least in the "highly interventionist" economies of today. Thus, what is perceived as an inequitable state of affairs is often the result of some particular group(s) of individuals' decision or action.

Hayek concentrates more or less completely on the equity of market rewards. He does not ridicule the sympathy we feel for human misery at large. Thus, while (in Hayek's view) social justice is nonsense when applied to market rewards, something much like it can have a meaning when applied to the 'after-the-market' distribution:

> There is no reason why in a free society government should not assure to all protection against severe deprivation in the form of an assured minimum income, or a floor below which nobody need to descend. To enter into such an insurance against extreme misfortune may well be to the benefit of all; or it may be felt to be a clear moral duty of all to assist, within the organized community, those who cannot help themselves. So long as as such a uniform minimum income is provided outside the market to all those who, for any reason, are unable to earn in the market an adequate maintenance, this need not lead to a restriction of freedom, or conflict with the Rule of Law. (p. 87)

The interesting question is: Why would (a free) society want to institute such a minimum income? Hayek's text is concerned with the lack of foundations for such considerations. Yet in this passage Hayek speaks of "moral obligation". One interpretation would be that when Hayek writes "social justice" he means the use of the term for other purposes; i.e., the furthering of the unjust purposes of some group of individuals. But the pages preceding the quoted passage do not support such an interpretation; he clearly does not approve of any concept of social justice. I can only conclude that Hayek has some place for equity considerations, he only calls them something else.[18] (For what could underlie such a passage other than the idea that it is not right for some people to be deprived?)

These passages indicate that Le Grand is right. Even Hayek can be read to admit the possibility of equity considerations. But I believe the non-spontaneity of modern Western economies, which Le Grand invokes to support his view, only weakly supports Le Grand's conclusion. A more promising path is offered by the view of justice as the existence of justified claims by some on others, i.e., of justice as a relation between individuals in society as opposed to justice as an attribute of actions. The passage on a guaranteed minimum income is an example of such a reasoning.

There remains the problem of how we should explain the difference between Hayek's ridiculing the concept of distributive justice on the one hand and his acceptance of minimum income considerations, on the other. Because, while the two are not identical, they are not unrelated either. Hayek's reason for guaranteeing a livelihood for those who are unable to provide for themselves, namely, the existence of moral claims and the acceptance of such claims by others, can readily be extended. Why should we not feel that the claims of the unemployed to unemployment insurance, young parents to maternity and paternity benefits and so on, in short, typical claims in the modern welfare state, are justified? And what, then, separates these claims from those supported by the 'social justice' Hayek so ardently criticizes?

After all, especially if one rejects what I have called mechanical decision procedures when faced with choices regarding distributive justice, the causes and consequences of the situation can not be ignored. Equality is not necessarily considered a good in itself, but something that leads to other goods. Semantics aside, what is really going on in redistributing income is the fulfillment of the moral obligations of some toward others.

---

[18]One could perhaps argue that it is a mistake to talk of society as a subject, that it is not society but some specific subject, such as the minister in charge of social affairs who brings about such a minimum income. But that is mixing semantics with the issue: why would income-maintenance programs be supported?

2 The cement of society and the extended order. A study of F. A. Hayek's functionalism

Ralf Eriksson

Introduction

As man, at least as far as western life-style is concerned, has grown more individualistic, more self-sufficient and more isolated from the direct dependence of the group, it may appear somewhat of a mystery that man lives in societies.[1] What invisible strings tie people together? Which forces have made possible the incredibly complex co-operation that is a precondition for the tremendous number of people – and also the technical miracles as well as the environmental destruction – that replenish the world of today? The answers are legion. By way of introduction, one answer which the independent thinker meeting people mainly in the market-place – strolling around the *agora* – might find natural would be money, or at a somewhat deeper level of explanation, self-interest. Another, perhaps not so independent a thinker may be enrolled in the army, and plausibly argue that the force keeping people together is coercion.

Perhaps the most thoroughgoing line of division – or should one say antagonism – within the social sciences is between 'mainstream' economics on one hand and other social sciences (and many of the humanities) on the other. Briefly, these differences in view may be characterized as follows. Economists tend to want to explain the existence of society as result of rational and selfish behaviour, while the latter groups' perspective is rather that rational and

---

[1]Of course this view requires a certain theoretical background. In practice society does not appear like a mystery.

selfish behaviour (among other kinds of behaviour) is the result of man's socialization into such features.

We may call the economist's view methodological individualism and the latter view methodological collectivism, but of course, there is more to distinguish economics from other social sciences than this methodological feature. A common definition – probably as good as any for my purposes – of economics circumscribes it as 'management and distribution of scarce resources between multiple needs'. The 'rest' of the society – the non-economic sphere – would thus be something that is not managed and is not concerned with scarce resources. Something that is not managed or manageable is, among other things, something which is not rationally calculable. This again can depend on many reasons: if there is no scarcity there can be no price. Other 'non-economic' reasons are perhaps more important in explaining the impossibility of 'rational management' or calculation in the social sphere. Some things could simply not be perceived as being economically measurable. E.g., we know that many people consider the value of life unmeasurable, so they would not kill anybody or sell a child at any price. On the other hand, we know that there are (sub-)cultures or circumstances in which such practices are accepted.[2]

Moral principles closely related to these are that we have things which are 'just done because they could not be done otherwise', or 'things which are just not done'. Often such action is not even reflected upon and answers like these are given to children (or economists or philosophers) who do not seem to have the acquired the required understanding. Insisting on having 'deeper answers' to this kind of moral questions may often be met with strong emotional reactions. Examples of these kinds of feelings/actions/non-actions are norms of 'decency' and 'proper behaviour', visible even in such every-day activity as clothing, table manners etc.

Under the 'non-economic residual' we then often use words like 'social', 'cultural', 'values', 'ethics', 'morals'. These words are commonly conceived as reflecting a more 'noble' side of human existence than the more 'earthly' 'economic'. Or so does much of the popular interpretation go.[3] At least the burden of proof is most often considered to be on the economic side, as far as the 'destructiveness' of economic values on non-economic values is considered. But on the other hand most economists are uninterested/incapable of defending themselves, often hiding under a scientific mask.

It should be evident from above that the limit between what is considered

---

[2]Thus we are told that you can hire a contract-killer in Estonia for some ten thousand marks, or that adoptions of babies in USA are 'facilitated' by payments to the biological mother.

[3]See Hirschman (1982).

the proper sphere of what is economically calculable and what is not, is not given once and for all, rather it is constantly in flux. But the change is hardly perceptible to the individual, tied to a certain time and place. It is commonly thought that the sphere of calculation has grown at the expense of traditionally 'moral spheres'. It should be remembered, however, that if this is the case, the direction of change has not been of a one-way nature only. Today we find the historical institutions of, say, selling letters of indulgence, reconciling crimes like murder by paying a fine or buying a wife quite repulsive if not outrightly wrong.[4]

Economics and 'simple' and 'meaningful' satisfaction?

Further, there is an additional dimension in the demarcation between what is economics and what is not, that I want to comment on. I think that it is not an overstatement to claim that there has been a tendency among social scientists and especially economists themselves to reduce economic choices to a mechanical action which is quite independent from its cultural context. I do not here mean only the strict optimizing approach in microeconomics textbooks, but the substantial emptiness which economists and perhaps also other social scientists tend to attribute to the economic agent. *Homo oeconomicus* seems to have to do with 'brute satisfaction' of *simple* (individualistic) biological needs while *homo sociologicus* is considered to be involved in the satisfaction of *meaningful* ('social') needs.[5]

Now I do not want to claim that such a distinction may not have its legitimate and adequate reasons and applications. It is in the nature of scientific idealization to overlook and/or isolate features which are to be seen as marginal to the phenomena to be described. Therefore it is in many cases quite motivated for economists to look at needs as 'given', that is, independent of their social formation. However, if one wants to study the interaction between the economic (calculating) and non-economic forms of reasoning and action, as is my intention here, one cannot be content with the existing division of labour between the social sciences. If we accept the distinction between 'simple' and 'meaningful' needs as a borderline between economics and 'non-economics' we will find that the field of economics – at least as an empirical discipline – will appear to have quite a limited area of application. Why is that?

---

[4]Cf. Simmel (1978, 355ff.).
[5]In this distinction I am basing myself on O'Hear's discussion of Oakeshott. See O'Hear (1992, 68).

An example of fulfillment of 'meaningful' *versus* 'simple' needs could be 'going to church' and 'eating' respectively. Going to church, or to dramatize a bit, going to a christening or a funeral is generally and commonly conceived of as sharing common feelings, beliefs, language, conventions, etc. And there is not much to be said about that.[6]

Eating, on the other hand, is often given as an example of the fulfillment of a simple need, or as an optimizing-problem considering the intake of calories, given your budget. However, upon a closer look it seems clear that even much of eating can be considered as a meaningful activity (which does not, of course, mean that all eating is of such kind). And here I am not thinking only of celebrations, holidays etc., but of ordinary meals. Besides broader cultural patterns of cooking every family has their own specific cultural traditions of meals, their secret recipes, table manners, clothing etc.

To all this one might say, with some reason, to be sure, that the modern 'commercial' culture has been destroying the mentioned traditions. Eating is in many cases no more as just described, but the family tradition has been replaced by, say, a pizza and a Coke.

Tempting as it would be to continue the discussion along these lines I will not do so here. However, one remark may be in place. The disappearance of the tradition does not mean that 'modern' – fast food – eating should be considered as satisfaction of brute animal needs, or as 'meaningless'. On the contrary, almost any attempt to bring to mind commercials on food and drink show at least to my memory that even the fulfillment of the most fundamental need, drinking, may have a lot of meaning, let it be with a considerable element of 'consumerism'. With this I mean that a lot of advertising seems to stress the social elements of belonging and togetherness.[7]

Nevertheless, as suggested above, to claim that economics can ignore fulfillment of meaningful needs or culture, would restrict economics to the study of how the sales of drinks or blankets varies with temperature. Only in such extremely simple cases can culture be taken *ceteris paribus* and consumption as fulfillment of a simple physiological need.

---

[6]This is not to deny that much churchgoing may be 'mere' empty conventions. That is why I chose to dramatize the example.

[7]'We want to teach the world to sing in perfect harmony' – as a result of consuming 'our brand', of course. What is perhaps the most problematic thing in this connection is that the meanings and values do not any more arise from within the community, but from advertising-companies, which are by no means creating values out of nothing, but rather exploiting the value meanings of tradition. In other connections the values may often represent elements which are totally alien to the culture into which they are implanted.

Economizing thinking and uniformity of value

Now, having said this, and even if we accept the view just referred to, we should not underestimate the importance of economic and economistic thinking. At least physically society consists of separate individuals which even if they are not mere atoms are not 'socially determined' either.[8] And economic practices and economic thinking – as well as any other form of culture – probably have had (and surely continue to have) a great effect upon people's self-image in this sense, and thus also on his behaviour, especially in western culture, as noted. It would therefore amount to outright daydreaming to ignore the role of the self-interested, individualistic character in modern society.

And in relation to the discussion above we may add that it is even possible to characterize the formation of economics itself as a discipline, as giving *a meaning* or social intelligibility to self-interest in the sense of conceiving of it as – not a damaging feature, as was taught by the church – but a feature that was beneficial for the whole society.

As should be fairly evident by now, I believe that it is not a fruitful strategy to put economic and non-economic values, reasoning and behaviour *categorically* against each other. Economizing is a form of and an offspring of culture itself. Even if it sometimes seems, as it were, that economizing is living a life of its own, we cannot say that economic values *as such* are any more dividing or uniting a force than non-economic ones when we study a given society.

To avoid misunderstanding this requires some words of clarification. Firstly, I do not have the slightest doubt that the modern economic calculating mind has played a very important role in the change and destruction of 'primitive' cultures to the degree that such are practically extinct from earth today.[9] And of course we are all in a sense either 'producers', 'products' or 'victims' of this culture, but the change was probably smoother for our ancestors than for relatively late confrontations with primitive cultures.

However, if we look at the process from the perspective of a *unification of values*, I think that calculative thinking has greatly contributed to this. In good and in bad, both in the creations or products of institutional character (say, as money) and (what seems to indiscernible from these) the increased

---

[8]We could say that the concept of 'free will', as shown so well e.g. by Dostoyevsky kicks in both directions. The free will individualizes man to the degree that he even refuses to act in his own best (economistic) interest. See also Frankfurt (1971).

[9]This is probably no exaggeration. In this connection I recall a newspaper notice which reported a study which predicted that 90 % of the world's languages will be extinct within the next hundred years.

income and standard of living. Against the background of the preceding
section we say say that the historical process has unified the means of making
action intelligible.

We will probably never know what was lost in this process, but the unification brought about by the uniformity of formerly different experience worlds,
separated by norms, religion, geographical distance, etc., is something very
few of us would feel we could be dispensed with. Here I am not primarily or
even mainly thinking about human artifacts, but above all about the modern
values of personal liberty, equality and other principal ideals that are so in-
timately connected with the spread of economizing, absurd as it may sound
to the modern ear. But this is only because the new economic order created
evils and problems of its own, which to us seem contradictory to these ideals.

Summing up this lengthy and ambivalent – to put it mildly[10] – introduction; the problem here is 'simply' a problem of balance. How can one keep in
mind the importance of economic categories, and at the same time balance
this view against the fact that these in themselves are social categories deeply
interwoven in the 'fabric of society', i.e. connected to other life-spheres by
having social meaning. This interaction has occupied the sharpest minds of
social science, such as Marx, especially in his early works (Marx 1967), Sombart (1902), Weber (1923), Durkheim (1984) and Simmel (1978) to mention
only some of the most outstanding. And even these outstanding thinkers
showed the human feature of 'falling into the decay' of the existing division
of labour.[11]

Hayek, functionalism and the 'Hayek problem'

However, the purpose if this chapter is not to attempt anything like a synthe-
sis between the above-mentioned original social thinkers. Nor am I primarily
attempting a comparison of economic and non-economic thinkers. The purpose is a more modest one: I will attempt a critical discussion of a single
social thinker; Friedrich Hayek.

The main reason for choosing Hayek as the theme in a study like this,
i.e. attempting to grasp something of the interaction between 'economy' and
'culture', is that Hayek is one of the few who seems to do justice to both

---

[10]Schizophrenic would in fact be a better word, I think, for the attitude of modern man
to these matters. As will be evident below this theme of 'schizophrenia' also runs through
Hayek's views on this matters.

[11]We may note that even Marx applied this division, devoting most of his time to develop
his pure economic analysis, despite his wider social philosophy.

points of view.[12]

A little differently expressed we may say with O'Hear (1992, 71) that Hayek in contrast to such thinkers as Oakeshott and Popper tries to answer why "some practices, institutions and traditions persist and others die out".

Now, as a matter of fact, Hayek has always been considered a bit of an 'angry man'[13] in the sense of going against the stream – also within economics. I think that the main controversies revolving around Hayek's work that are of interest to the theme of this chapter have been concerned with: (a) his methodological individualism and, (b) his persistent and devoted advocacy of the market order.

Briefly put, it is the purpose of this chapter to show that, contrary to popular opinion and much earlier interpretation of Hayek, these features do not seem to acquire any central role when we consider Hayek's social philosophy as a whole. This does not mean that the earlier interpretations were wrong, but rather that Hayek's own views have changed to the degree that the position of the features of methodological individualism and extreme pro-market attitude in Hayek's system must be reassessed.

Against the background of the preceding sections, but little more specifically expressed, the argument in this chapter is meant to go as follows. After describing the concepts of 'methodological individualism' and the 'invisible hand (mechanism) of the market', as Hayek applies them, I will argue that the invisible hand mechanism can be given a functionalist interpretation. Concretely, this means that I claim that economizing behaviour can be explained *by* the function it has for the market mechanism. Of course, any need to explain economizing behaviour does not arise within neoclassical economics, because it is *postulated.*

According to Hayek's thinking, economizing behaviour must in itself be in need of explanation because Hayek does not *a priori* assume that man is *homo oeconomicus.* On the contrary Hayek postulates that primitive man is the opposite; a social and altruistic creature. Therefore, seen in the evolutionary perspective, as Hayek does, there must exist (an evolutionary) gap between the behaviour and reasoning of 'primitive social man' and that of 'modern

---

[12]Lest it should be claimed that such a thing is an impossibility, it is perhaps better to say that he seems – especially in his later works – to *try* to do justice. In fact, 'to do justice' is a vague expression, for what Hayek really attempts is to show the synergetic interdependence between culture and economy. A bit differently expressed Hayek formulates the basic question in his *Fatal Conceit* as "how does our morality emerge, and what implications may its mode of coming into being have for our economic and political life?" (Hayek 1988, 8).

[13]Both as young and as old, although perhaps less as an old man, as his appreciation grew with the awarding of the Nobel Memorial Price and the decline of the socialist system.

economic man'. This problem I will call the *Hayek problem of the evolution of human culture.*

I will then try to show that it is possible, at least in principle, to solve this problem with the aid of Hayek's works by constructing what could be termed 'functional cycles'. With this I mean a describing system of the function and the institution (the behavioral trait). The combination of such cycles can then, in principle at least, be used to solve the Hayek problem.

I then proceed to make some comments about the element of *verstehen* and meaning in Hayek's functionalism, which seems to be in conflict with his methodological individualism. Finally I make some concluding remarks on Hayek's functionalism and the relation between this and the ethics of his 'market-mindedness'.

Methodological individualism?

But before it is possible to understand Hayek's general views we must say something about what distinguishes his methodological individualism from his fellow economists'. In fact the ordinary economist does not give very much of a motivation for his methodological individualism. As a motivational statement the classical economist is usually content with the 'assumption of given, stable preferences for the individual agent' etc.[14]

Of course, Hayek's use of the term also implies that explanation in social science should be based on the individual and not take as its starting point some kind of 'organic unity'. However, as we shall see just below, his individualism does not imply reductionism. In fact, it can be questioned how consequent Hayek's methodological individualism really is. Hodgson (1991) has shown, in my view quite convincingly, that Hayek's view could rather be termed 'group-selection'. Related to this is Hayek's epistemology (cf. the economists assumption of 'perfect information'). Let Hayek speak for himself:

> Till Science has literally completed its work and not left the slightest unexplained residue in man's intellectual processes, the facts of our mind remain not only data to be explained but also data on which the explanation of human action guided by those mental phenomena must be based[...]The question is here not how far man's picture of the external world fits the facts, but how by his actions, determined by the views and concepts he possesses, man

---

[14]Often more for the sake of tractability than anything else.

builds up *another world* of which the individual becomes a part. And by "the views and concepts people hold" we do not mean merely their knowledge of external nature. We mean all they know and believe about themselves, other people and the external world, in short everything which determines their actions, including science. This is the field to which the social studies or the "moral sciences" addresses themselves. (Hayek 1942, 276)(italics added)

I think already this passage puts important restrictions upon the methodological individualism of Hayek. First of all, the individual or the 'social atom' does not act upon some (un-)imageable objective knowledge of the world, but only upon how he perceives it. This may sound tautological, but compare this again with the neoclassical assumption of 'perfect information'.

Secondly, and related to this, note that 'man builds up another world' should of course not be taken as he was living in a completely illusory world, but rather that he shares views and beliefs, a common frame of reference with other people. The correspondence to the external nature is not important in Hayek's view but exactly the characteristic that the beliefs are shared. Briefly, the beliefs and knowledge of the 'man-built world' – i.e. the features of *intersubjectivity* – would be both unnecessary and impossible to have for a single, isolated individual. This is exactly the same feature that was named meaning in the section above.

Thirdly, we have the point of non-reductionism; to be human, i.e. to be able to see actions as *meaningful* is an advantage, not a disadvantage, when studying societies.[15] In this connection it may be noted that Hayek also attributes *verstehen* to Karl Menger, one of his foremost predecessors:

'Observation', as Menger uses the term, has thus a meaning that modern behaviourists would not accept; and it implies a *Verstehen* ('understanding') in the sense in which Max Weber later developed the concept. It seems to me that there is still much that could be said in defense of the original position of Menger (and of the Austrians generally) on this issue. (Hayek 1990, 277)

Within 'mainstream economics' *Verstehen* is not considered to have any role. We shall return to non-reductionism and *verstehen* at the end of the chapter.

---

[15]Hayek approvingly quotes Demokritos in this connection "$\alpha\nu\theta\rho\omega\pi\sigma\varsigma\ \epsilon\sigma\tau\iota\nu\ o\ \pi\alpha\nu\tau\epsilon\varsigma\ \iota\delta\mu\epsilon\nu$" ("Man is what is known to all") (Hayek 1943, 63).

Hayek's economics

1. The invisible hand

Perhaps it is about time we should start where Hayek started himself; with economics. However, this is not the place to give an overview of his economic works. Only the very general principles will be given in so far as they are essential for giving a background for the understanding of his general social philosophy.

Already a superficial acquaintance with Hayek's work gives the impression that one of the most common terms is 'spontaneous order' – in one form or another.[16] The following passage was picked at random:[17]

> I am convinced that if [the price mechanism] were the result of deliberate human design, and if people guided by the price changes understood that their decisions have significance far beyond their immediate aim, this mechanism would have been acclaimed as one of the greatest triumphs of the human mind. Its misfortune is the double one that it is not the product of human design and that the people guided by it usually do not know why they are made to do what they do.

The Hayekian spontaneous order is the 'collective' result of individuals acting on whatever motivations they happen to have (as implicated by methodological individualism). However in the individuals' intentions or motives the achievement of the overall result has no part. And what is more, even if the overall result would be a deliberate part of people's intentions this would not lead to a better result, but to a worse one. The deliberate striving for the common good would distract you from doing what you are most suited for – using your 'particular knowledge of time and space' - and so decrease the overall effectiveness of the system. Furthermore, with the complex division of labour we have today you cannot have an overview of what the common good is (Cf. Hayek (1988, 81)).

Indeed, according to Hayek's methodological individualism, this 'result of individual action but not of design' (this spontaneous order, these unintended consequences, this invisible hand, to name some synonyms) is also the

---

[16]Hayek lately seems to have agreed that terms like 'self-generating order' or 'self-organizing structures' in the vein of cybernetics. Cf. Hayek (1982a, xvii-xix).

[17](Hayek 1949, 87) This example is of course not completely random. Still it says something that the passage was obtained by 'first trial', selecting the nearest book by Hayek on my shelf and opening a page at random and reading down the same page. The term 'spontaneous order' did not appear but the concept itself did.

raison d'etre for economic science and social science in general. Of course, if consequences would correspond to intentions there would be very little to explain.

Perhaps the most important features of the 'self-sufficiency' – both as a normative and a positive point – of the market in Hayek's view should be given here. These points of view are strongly interrelated.

2. The problem of knowledge

Hayek repeatedly stresses the feature that the market 'computes' the nonscientific knowledge, i. e. knowledge of particular time and place. The central feature for the market is not that of self-interest but,

> [f]ar more important than this moral attitude which might be regarded as changeable [...] is the constitutional limitation of man's knowledge and interests, the fact that he *cannot* know more than a tiny part of the whole society. (Hayek 1949, 14)

The market, just because this knowledge is particular, can *transcend* and *extend* any individual knowledge and is in effect the 'tool' that knits the different knowledge together. It is in Hayek's view "[t]he curious task of economics is to demonstrate to men how little they really know about what they imagine they can design (Hayek 1988, 76)". The problem with trying to design a price-mechanism is that it destroys or eliminates the particular knowledge and replaces it with a general, scientific one, thus leading to a loss in information that may had benefited the society.

And the general role of the market of spreading information more effectively than other social systems should not be forgotten (cf. the discussion about the 'uniformity of value' above):

> Competition is essentially a process of the formation of opinion: by spreading information, it creates that unity and coherence of the economic system which we presuppose when we think of it as one market. (Hayek 1949, 106)

3. Economics should be interpreted as catallactics

According to Hayek one of the great confusions within economics is caused by this term itself. The problem is that 'economics' is used both in the original Aristotelian meaning of 'prudent housekeeping' and as a word for the spontaneous order (cosmos) which this results in. As the proper word for this spontaneous order Hayek proposes *catallactics* from the Greek word *katallassein* or *katallatein*.[18]

In the perspective of Hayek's life-work this neologism is understandable. In the long debate concerning 'socialist calculation' (Hayek 1949, 119-208) the pre-eminent issue seems to have evolved around the present terminological dichotomy.

If there did not exist any difference between economics as 'prudent house-keeping' and 'economics as exchange', the problems of economics could in fact be reduced to engineering-problems. Consider

> the industrial engineer who decides on the best method of produc-
> tion of a given commodity on the basis of given prices is concerned
> only with technological problems, although he may speak of his
> trying to find the most economical method. But the only element
> which makes his decision *in its effects* an economic one is not any
> part of his calculations but the fact that he uses, as a basis for
> these calculations, prices as he finds them on the market. (Hayek
> 1949, 122)

Someone might be tempted to insist here that the engineer does not get the price from the market but from the price-list of his subcontractor, who got his price from his subcontractor, etc., and then all could eventually be based on some fundamental (labour?) value. But of course this is not to state an economic problem, which always presupposes the problem of choosing.

Suppose instead that our engineer has to decide not to produce only one product but several. With scarce resources (i.e. a given factory) this means that a choice to produce more of one good is simultaneously a choice to produce less of another good. How is the proportion of quantities of different goods to be determined? It can be effectively determined only by calculating the economic advantage that is lost by producing a certain amount of the other good, in which decision our engineer must rely on the market(-price of the good and its inputs). Of course the relative quantities *can* be determined in some other way (political preferences, throwing dice, *fingerspitzgefühl* etc.), but this would not lead to the best *economic* result (other than by coincidence).

It is perhaps correct to say that in Hayek's view the economic problem could never be solved 'technically', e.g. by computers and operations analysis, but only by a market consisting of real, human agents.

---

[18](Hayek 1982b, 108); (Hayek 1990, 90); (Hayek 1988, 112). Hayek's enthusiasm for the word may derive from the fact that it does not only mean 'to exchange' but also 'receive into the community' and 'to turn from enemy into a friend' (Hayek 1990, 90).

4. The market is a process

The problems described above would perhaps be not so severe if we were living in 'static world', e.g. some kind of stationary state or feudalism. The problems of ignorance would largely disappear, catallactics would converge towards prudent housekeeping. But whatever the merits or dismerits of such a world would be, it is not a picture of *this* world. As for Hayek, he has consequently during his career stressed the non-static, if not anti-static, nature of competition:

> [T]he practice of referring to 'the existing state of knowledge', and to information available to acting members of a market process either as 'data' or as 'given' (or even by the pleonasm of 'given data') often leads economists to assume that this knowledge exists not merely in dispersed form but that the whole of it might be available to some single mind. This conceals the character of competition as a discovery procedure. (Hayek 1988, 98-99)

In numerous places Hayek maintains that "we do not know in advance the facts that determine the actions of competitors"[19]. Neither is the assumption – usually regarded as harmless – of consumers holding a stable preference ordering, known to producers, compatible with Hayek's process view of the world: "which goods are scarce goods, or which things are goods, and how scarce and valuable they are – these are precisely the things which competition has to discover" (Hayek 1990, 181).

In a sense, much of Hayek's *economic* work is a magnificent elucidation of Adam Smith's concept of of the invisible hand according to which individual self-interest will (counter-intuitively) lead to the best overall result. And of course, many of these characteristics of Hayek he shares with the other members of the so called Austrian school of economics; especially Karl Menger and Ludwig von Mises frequently occur as references in his work. However, as we shall see below, what gives Hayek his own special features is the greater system into which the above features are incorporated. We can also say that we will learn more of his view of economics when we take this larger system into consideration.

---

[19]See e.g. Hayek (1990, 179-190).

Functionalism and the invisible hand

Well, one may say, but do these characteristics have anything to do with
the initial questions we started with? What is it that ties people together
in a society? Does not the existence of a spontaneous order imply that the
cement of the society is made of self-interest? To answer this questions we
must step back, in fact to Adam Smith again.

Let us think about Adam Smith's formulation of the principle of the
'invisible hand'. The 'invisible' here is the link between the individual actions
and motives and the unintended overall effects. If economic science has
fulfilled its role as stated by Hayek and others it must be able to explain
the mechanism that exists between individual actions and the unintended
consequences or pattern of these. What kind of candidates do we have for
this mechanism? Is for example the Theory of General Equilibrium a possible
one? At least as far as Hayek is concerned it seems safe to say 'no'. General
Equilibrium Theory shows, on the basis of a few rationality assumptions, that
equilibrium (i.e. neither excess demand nor supply) can exist on all markets
at the same time.[20] This can not be compatible with Hayek's view of the
invisible hand mechanism: (a) because it relies on *homo oeconomicus'* strict
rationality, a feature which Hayek does not subscribe to[21] and, (b) General
Equilibrium Theory does not describe a process in time, but is essentially
static. As just noted this is not Hayek's way of looking at the market.

Let me propose an interpretation of Hayek's (and perhaps other's) invisible hand, which seems quite natural in view of Hayek's image of the market
process, an interpretation which will seem even more reasonable when we
consider Hayek's whole system. I would say that the most fitting description
of Hayek's view of the market process as well as of his general social philosophy is functionalism.[22] I.e. for Hayek the cement of the society is in my
view best describable as and by functionalism.

So let us start with the market process and then proceed towards an increased complication of Hayek's system. My interpretation of 'functionalism'
stems from Elster (1985). As Elster shows, functionalism as used by some
anthropologists, has led to the interpretation of almost any form of behaviour
or institution as 'functional', i.e. vital for the existence of the society in question. As a remedy for this tautological character Elster proposes 5 criteria

---

[20]For details see e.g. Arrow and Hahn (1971).

[21]See discussion above, p. 37.

[22]That Hayek could and should be interpreted as a functionalist has been proposed at
least by Ullman-Margalit (1978) and Walker (1986, 44-45). After writing this chapter
I have noted that Hodgson (1993) has also attributed functionalistic features to Hayek.
Unfortunately, I have not been able to consider the views of Hodgson here.

for explanations to count as 'truly' functionalist in the social sciences. Let me for the sake of clarity repeat these (Elster 1985, 57-58):

Cycle 1.   The basic criteria for functionalism

An institution or a behavioural pattern X is explained by its function Y for group Z if and only if:

1. Y is an effect of X.
2. Y is beneficial for Z.
3. Y is unintended by the actors producing X.
4. Y – or at least the causal relation between X and Y – is unrecognized by the actors in Z.
5. Y maintains X by a causal feedback loop passing through Z.

According to Elster there are only a few cases of successful application – i.e. one that fulfills all these criteria – of functionalism within the social sciences.[23] Usually some of the arguments, most often (5), is forgotten from a proposed functional explanation. The best known of successful functional explanations, according to Elster, is by the 'Chicago school' of economics to explain profit-maximizing as a result of natural selection. If X is set to 'rules of thumb' and Y to 'profit-maximization' and Z to the 'group of firms', natural selection will secure that non-profit maximizing rules of thumb will be extinct, while firms with profit-maximizing rules will prosper.[24]

Now, let us as a further illustration look at another example that is slightly different from this: denote by Y 'the market', by X 'selfish and rational behaviour' (economizing behaviour) and by Z 'the group' participating in the market. Let us then see if the mechanism fullfils the requirements of functionalism.

---

[23]See however Douglas (1986) for an application of Elster's argument as well as for criticism of it.

[24]Elster notes that such an explanation will be a successful (functional) only if the maximizing rules of thumb are spread among the firms as a result of take-overs and not as a result of imitation (in which case it would not satisfy (4)). However, as far as I can see organizational practices may well be spread by imitation without understanding the causal relation between these and profit-maximization.

Cycle 2. Explanation of self-interested behaviour

1. Y (the market mechanism) is an effect of X (self-interested behaviour).
2. Y is beneficial for Z (by making exchange more efficient through e.g. specialization).
3. Y is ('by definition') unintended by X; The intention with X is to satisfy personal needs and desires, not to bring about a market.
4. The actors (Z) do not recognize the causal relation between self-interested behaviour and the market.
5. The market mechanism (Y) maintains self-interested behaviour (X) by 'rewarding' self-interested and rational agents in the market participating group (Z).

Clearly economizing behaviour fulfills the criteria for functional explanation and it is explained by its market function. However, we may think of at least two objections to this explanation. Some would perhaps want to reverse X and Y and look at selfish behaviour as an effect of the market. I do not deny that this can be the case, but it is beside my main point here. Moreover this relation is taken care of by the feedback loop in (5). Another related intuitive reaction would be that self-interest and economizing behaviour is in no need for explanation. However, to start a discussion of economists' motivation for selfish and rational behaviour would lead to a story of its own. Anyway, one can surely say that economists have felt no pressing need to explain economizing behaviour. On the contrary, of course, this seems quite an awkward way to describe the thinking of a mainstream economist, who typically takes economizing as *given*. In other words, it is the market that is considered the explanandum, not *homo oeconomicus*.

However, against both objections I maintain that the proposed interpretation – i.e. in the functional explanation above – is the classical one in economics. It is, I think, quite possible to see a quite 'pure' functionalism already in Smith, when he seeks a 'meaning' for self-interest. Let me digress for a moment to Smith, not as a *curiosum* but because it is important for the general understanding of the actual concepts here, and that it is evident that Smith greatly affected Hayek on this point. We need only consider the following comments by Smith concerning the invisible hand:

[E]very thing is contrived for advancing the two great purposes of nature, the support of the individual, and the propagation of the species. Smith (1976, 87)

[The rich, in spite of their natural selfishness] are led by an invisible hand to make nearly the same distribution of the necessaries of life, which would have been made, had the earth been divided into equal portions among all its inhabitants, and thus without intending it, without knowing it, advance the interest of the society, and afford means to the multiplication of the species. (Smith 1976, 184-185)

Self-interest has a function for the group, otherwise it would not exist, and this function is the market-invisible-hand (-mechanism) – which is beneficial for those engaging in it. We have no difficulty in tracing the requirements for a functional explanation from this passage although Smith's arguments differ a bit from 'modern functionalism':

(1) The invisible hand (i.e. the market-mechanism) is an effect of selfishness. We cannot in detail reconstruct Smith's argument here, but bluntly put it goes as follows. Smith's problem as a moral philosopher was the vice of selfishness (or self-interest). How could such a thing which the great religious authorities had condemned be permitted to exist. Basing himself on Mandeville and the functionalist truistic conviction of the first passage above Smith could convince himself that Mandeville's virtue of selfishness could not have caused so much "alarm among those who are the friends of better principles, had it not in some respects bordered upon the truth" (Smith 1976, 313). This means that selfishness can be seen as the power which puts the invisible (beneficial) hand into work. We may also express this as that the *meaning* of selfishness – for Smith – was to be found in the existence of the invisible hand.

That requirement (2) must be valid for Smith is evident. As in the example of the invisible hand above it is beneficial in equalizing incomes.

Requirement (3) is of course also valid. The rich in Smith's example have no intention whatsoever to help the poor, only to satisfy their own selfish desires.

(4) The actors do not, in Smith's view, recognize the causal relation between their behaviour and the invisible hand: they, "without intending it, without knowing it, advance the interest of the society".

Requirement (5) is (as could be expected) the one that is most unclearly stated by Smith. However, I do not think we have to use force to make his thoughts compatible with the requirement. Referring here only to the above example of the invisible hand, Smith clearly invokes a psychologically – and deceptive – rewarding feedback-mechanism.[25]

The Hayek problem

Coming back to Hayek we may add a further reason for wanting to explain economizing behaviour (by the market function). He explicitly considers self-interested or economizing behaviour in itself in need of explanation, because this is in his view an alien element in 'primitive man'. According to Hayek, primitive man is not selfish but rather he is altruistic and 'social'.

> The primitive individualism described by Thomas Hobbes is hence a myth. The savage is not solitary, and his instinct is collectivist. There was never a "war of all against all".[26]

On the other hand, as Hayek emphasizes[27] 'modern' man seems clearly to be endowed with characteristics like self-interest and rationality, otherwise we would have great problems with the functioning of the invisible hand.

> Part of our present difficulty is that we must constantly adjust our lives, our thoughts and our emotions, in order to live simultaneously within different kinds of orders according to different rules. If we were to apply the unmodified, uncurbed, rules of the micro-cosmos (i.e., of the small band or troop, or of, say, our families) to the macro-cosmos (our wider civilisation), as our instincts and sentimental yearnings often make us wish to do, *we would destroy it*. Yet if we were always to apply the rules of the extended order to our more intimate groupings, *we would crush them*. So we must learn to live in two sorts of world at once. To apply the name 'society' to both, or even to either, is hardly of any use, and can be most misleading. (Hayek 1988, 18)

This passage very well reveals the basic dialectic of the *Fatal Conceit*, and much of Hayek's other later work as well. Hayek goes as far as to call

[25]Because of the alleged deceptiveness I am no quite sure that it fully satisfies condition (5), but it must come quite near: "The pleasures of wealth and greatness [...] strike the imagination as something grand and beautiful and noble, of which the attainment is well worth all the toil and anxiety which we are so apt to bestow on it. And it is well that nature imposes upon us in this manner. It is this deception which rouses and keeps in continual motion the industry of mankind." (Smith 1976, 183)

[26](Hayek 1988, 12), cf. e.g. Hayek (1990, 8-9).

[27]See section 'Hayek's economics and the invisible hand'.

this conflict in man's 'two natures' "perhaps the major theme of the history of civilisation" (Hayek 1988, 18).

I interpret Hayek, in the light of this, as that there must have occurred a change in the behavioral patterns – and more generally speaking in their world view, of course – of men. There seems to be, if not a paradox, then a problem here; how can a creature that is by nature altruistic and social turn into a self-interested one? This problem I have called the *Hayek problem* (of cultural evolution).

What possible candidates do we have for the explanation of the Hayek problem? Firstly, an explanation building on genetic selection must be rejected. On no account can we here be doing with genetic change because of the minimal time span (a few thousand years), speaking in terms of biological change. The explanation to the Hayek problem must thus be searched for in cultural change, or cultural evolution.

Now, considering this, note that as such there is nothing in the formulation of the functional explanation above which would explain the formation or *genesis* of economizing behaviour (and the market function). It just describes the maintenance, or *raison d'etre* of the mechanism once it has arisen but not *why* it has arisen in the first place. (cf. Ullman-Margalit (1978, 149) and Langlois (1987, 249–251)). Or we might express this by saying that the genesis of the mechanism can also be 'explained' *provided* that we assume economizing behaviour as an initial characteristic. As just described, Hayek's position is the opposite one; that economizing is a learned characteristic.

Thus, in accordance with Ullman-Margalit, I conclude that to have a complete explanation, we must to the above five criteria – the story of functional maintenance – add a story of origin.[28]

Accordingly, when Hayek claims that "the problem of origin or formation and that of the manner of functioning of social institutions was essentially the same" (Hayek 1967, 101), I believe it is contradictory to his own evolutionary theory. Hayek's claim may be correct e.g., for Menger's theory of money, but Ullman-Margalit (1978) and Langlois (1987) give examples where the maintaining mechanism is different from the originative mechanism. I think that it is possible to claim that Hayek himself in the present case applied a distinction between the two types of explanations. Another way to express this would be to say that, in the light of Hayek's own work, the above example

---

[28]A story of origin – in fact belonging to the folklore of economics – would be that the market has always existed, or rather whenever two people meet, say in the desert, we have a market. The two people have different needs and different endowments and the higgle-haggle immediately begins, etc.. But the fact is also that this view causally rests on the assumption of the universal existence of *homo oeconomicus* and an assumption of common culture. Be that as it may, it is not compatible with Hayek's evolutionary conception.

of the market mechanism as a functional explanation for self-interest is a
necessary but not a *sufficient* explanation for the *development* of the market
order.

Morals and the extended order

As a matter of fact, Hayek was not – especially in his later works – content
with the explanation of the invisible hand or the market order in a restricted
sense. He talked about the whole civilization as the 'extended order'. I think
this reflects his increasing awareness of the importance of the non-economic
sphere in society. The 'extended order' is a spontaneous order or a self-
organizing structure that "arose from unintentionally conforming to certain
traditional and largely *moral* practices" (Hayek 1988, 6). This is clearly a
generalized form of the concept of market as an unintended consequence of
individual economizing behaviour. What I understand Hayek is saying is
that rational market-behaviour must clearly be encapsulated in a larger web
of social behaviour, and that both the market (following from economizing)
and non-market form (following from moral behaviour) of unintended consequences are needed.

Now, considering the Hayek problem, I think it might be solved within the
functional frame of reference. Hayek himself does not pretend to give a full
account of the evolution of the primitive, altruistic society to the 'extended
order'. However, I would claim that a fairly clear idea of its development can
be derived from his works.

The (key to understand the) missing link between 'instinct' (i.e., the social
features of 'primitive man) and 'the extended order' is the development of
rules, i.e., cultural and moral evolution. Before trying to explicate these
features let us first clarify Hayek's views on 'morals'.

He distinguishes between three kinds of morals.[29] Firstly we have the 'innate morality', which is the instinctive morality just mentioned (solidarity,
altruism). Of course, this morality cannot sustain the 'extended order', because it is thought to distract people from self-interest information-gathering
which is so essential for the effectiveness of the system.

The second form of morality is the "constructivist contention that an adequate morality can be designed and constructed afresh by reason" (Hayek
1988, 70), i.e. systems of morals, or ethics. It seems to me that this type
of morals in Hayek's view can only have a destructive impact. This is because there is always a loss in the available information compared to the

---

[29]Cf. Hayek (1990, 8-9).

body of morals that has spontaneously arisen when this is replaced by an artificial body designing moral rules; "[m]an did not adopt new rules of conduct because he was intelligent. He became intelligent by submitting to new rules of conduct" (Hayek 1982c, 163). This feature is exactly parallel to Hayek's stressing of the importance of pro-grassroots-con-authority information within the market.

Thirdly we have the 'evolved morality' (e.g. savings behaviour, private (several) property, honesty) that stands 'between instinct and reason', which obviously is supposed to 'tie together' – in the evolutionary process – the primitive and the modern man.[30]

Functionalist explanation of the formation of the extended order

Now, in the following sketch of a solution to the Hayek problem by means of a functionalist model it should be understood that I am doing this as a form of 'ideal type' explanation. In other words, what I try to do is not to explain the whole 'form of morality' but only to lay bare and study the change by means of its essential elements. A construction of a 'waterproof' link between 'primitive' and 'modern' morals is far beyond the purpose of this chapter.

Accordingly, what I am looking for here is a bridge between the two men 'primitive altruistic' and the 'modern self-interested' – a (functional) story about how man could overcome his natural instincts shaped for the primitive society and develop a mental constitution which was 'fit for' the extended order. I will now try to reconstruct the simple elements of this.

Now, Hayek's cycle is evidently to be based on the concepts of *order* and *rule*. Take Elster's five criteria and set X='rule' and Y='order'. Then we get Cycle 3.

---

[30]So we may in passing note that it must be evident from this that contrary to what has been claimed (Hodgson 1991), Hayek does not (at least in his later writings) claim that there is a 'true, unhampered market'.

Cycle 3. Hayek's basic functional pattern

A *rule* is explained by its *order* (for a group) if and only if:

1. The *order* is an effect of the *rule*.
2. The *order* is beneficial for the group.
3. The *order* is unintended by the actors producing the rule.
4. The *order* – or at least the causal relation between the *rule* and the *order* – is unrecognized by the actors.
5. The *order* maintains the *rule* by a causal feedback loop passing through the group.

Indeed, to call this scheme general is no exaggeration. However, it seems clear that this is just what Hayek intended it to be, involving both moral and market order, as well as other 'suborders'. But to get something out of the scheme we must fill it in with something less general. A slightly less general cycle would be the following, which explains the instinctive or innate morality (Hayek's 'first form' of morality).

Cycle 4. Explanation of rules of solidarity

1. The *Innate order* is an effect of the *rules of solidarity*.
2. The *Innate order* is beneficial for the group.
3. The *Innate order* is unintended by the actors producing *solidarity rule*.
4. The *Innate order* – or at least the causal relation between the *solidarity rule* and the *Innate order* – is unrecognized by the actors.
5. The *Innate order* maintains the *solidarity rule* by a causal feedback loop passing through the group.

Since this may give the impression of explaining one thing with itself (solidarity by solidarity rules or something similar) this cycle requires some explanation.[31] The misconception may arise here because this may be understood to be an uninteresting case of social explanation because the reasoning

---

[31]Note e.g. Hayek's way of 'defining' innate morality: "the innate morality, so-called, of our instincts (solidarity, altruism, group decision, and such like)" (Hayek 1988, 70).

is straightforward. If man is social, altruistic, solidaristic, etc., the overall result cannot be but a social, 'good' result. This may lead to an 'overdetermination' of this thought i.e. that 'primitive man' *planned* to be good *and because* of the overall good consequences. It is of course true that intended consequences are easier to understand than unintended, but Hayek's view here is that the consequences *are* unintended. The social order which evolves from the instinctive, social rules is in Hayek's view no more the product of reason than the function and order in an ant-heap (and neither is the extended order). In any case, I think at least the requirements (1)-(4) are satisfied in the view of this unintendedness. Primitive man did not understand the relation between his instinctive caring behaviour and the social order of the family, clan or tribe. Considering requirement (5) it seems clear to me that Hayek was confident, on biological grounds, that the innate order could better guarantee the survival of their children than 'selfish groups' would have.[32]

As should be clear by now, my main purpose is the reconstruction of Hayek's system. Indeed, such a reconstruction has been proposed by Hayek himself as "rational reconstruction" of "how the system came into being" (Hayek 1988, 69). However, this proposal did not consider Hayek's own ideas.

Now, what I propose is that the Hayek problem (as described in this functional form) may be 'solved' by showing how one can come from Cycle 4 (which describes the primitive society) to Cycle 2 (which describes the market society). Let me shortly outline how I conceive that this could be done.

Firstly, it should be noted that even if Hayek does not give anything like a full description of how the conflict between the innate order and the emanated order could be solved. However, I think it is fair to say that he gives a clear clue to that.

This happens mainly in a short appendix to the *'Fatal Conceit'*. Here Hayek enthusiastically mentions superstition as a factor which may be helpful in understanding the preservation of tradition.[33] Thus Hayek says that

> the effect of tabooing a thing [was] to endow it with a supernatu-
> ral or magical energy that rendered it practically unapproachable

---

[32]Whether or not Hayek was correct in this assumption is a controversial biological issue that I will not go into here. I will not take a stand here about whether Hayek's theory is right or wrong, i.e. how it can overcome the 'Hawk-Dove-problem', or the problem of opportunistic behaviour. For a discussion of these questions, see Hodgson (1993).

[33]Hayek: "I wish I could reprint the whole of [James Frazer's *Psyche's Task*] 84 pages as an illustrative appendix to this volume" (Hayek 1988, 157).

> by any but the owner. Thus taboo became a powerful instrument
> for strengthening the ties [...] of private property.[34]

It is notable that Hayek here gives a 'subjectivistic' explanation of the
preservation of tradition, and thus comes back to his main themes from *Scientism and the Study of Society*. The social world is what man intersubjectively
believes it is.[35] Realisticness of belief is not at all a point in case here. It
does not matter if peoples' beliefs are based on a belief that trees live or in
a monotheistic God. The point is the evolutionary effectiveness which the
rules that these beliefs sustain leads to.

Now, it is of course not the case that the possible strengthening (by taboo)
of private property immediately introduced the market or anything like it.
It must be remembered that in Hayek's view the 'social instincts' are always
with us. Rather Hayek's view would be something like the following.

We may with good reason think that e.g. superstition would be a disadvantage for a single individual. However, from the point of view of group
selection[36] it might be an advantage because of many reasons of varying
'functional' kind. Hayek's main example is that it encourages private property by which the group gets an advantage over other ones, perhaps through
better care of tools and weapons (Hayek 1988, 30).

We may express this line of thought as a functional cycle as follows. Now
the function (order, Y) is of course private property, and the behavioural
pattern (institution, rule, X) is superstition.[37]

---

[34](Hayek 1988, 157), quoting Frazer, see note below. Cf. also Hayek (1982a, 75) and
Hayek (1982c, 161).

[35]E.g. "only what people know or believe can enter as a motive into their conscious
action" (Hayek 1942, 284).

[36]Which conception is not, it must be admitted, totally uncontroversial. Hodgson
(1991), basing himself on modern biology, has remarked that one inconsistency in Hayek's
theory of group-selection is that it does not give a reason why selection could not work on
a higher level than groups, i.e. different economic systems. If selection is allowed to work
on a higher level also, then Hayek's view of the uncompromising centrality of the market
is in trouble. However, I will not develop this point here.

[37]Of course we would still have to explain where superstition comes from. I will assume
here that superstition is a 'natural trait' for all (primitive) people, an assumption I take
Hayek implicitly makes.

Cycle 5.   Superstition explained by its function for private
property

1.   *Private property* is an effect of *superstition.*
2.   *Private property* is beneficial for the group.
3.   *Private property* is unintended by the actors 'producing' *superstition.*
4.   *Private property* – or at least the causal relation between the *superstition* and *private property* – is unrecognized by the actors.
5.   *Private property* maintains *superstition* by a causal
feedback loop passing through the group.

Considering Hayek's assumptions the fulfillment of these requirements
should be fairly easy to see. Of course superstition as such does not create
private property at once, but again we must see this cycle working under
a long period and note that superstition creates the rules which makes private property possible. In this sense private property is an indirect effect of
superstition.

Likewise, it should also go without saying that for (2) that private property is indirectly beneficial in the long run. E.g. the magic characteristics
attributed to hunting weapons makes the maker/owner take better care of
these than otherwise. The magical characteristics make other members of
the tribe respect the maker/owners sole right to the weapon.[38] In such ways
private property may benefit the group.

However, it is also possible that ownership was concentrated to a few
and this made possible the accumulation of wealth and central government
as in the ancient civilizations. In such a situation private ownership is also
beneficial in the sense that such cultures were extremely more effective (in
war etc.) then people with a more egalitarian ownership. However, such
historical examples show that the road to the market and the extended order
is by no means a straight one. I will, however, not pursue this interesting
theme here.

(3) It is clear without saying that by no means can the intent with prac-
tising magic be the production of private property.[39]

___

[38]It may also be that the magical characteristics may induce the use of rites and rituals in
making weapons, which may be essential for guaranteeing a uniform technological quality
of these.

[39]Of course superstition can and has been used to bolster private property. I discuss

(4) In the same way it seems clear that the causal relation between superstition and property cannot be known. It is quite obvious that once such a relation could be known, superstition can no more function as such.

Of course (5) is again the most critical point. In what sense can private property maintain superstition if requirements (3) and (4) are to hold? The obvious connection between superstition and private property is in the same sense as Marx talks about religion as the opium for the people. But of course Marx here sees religion as a part of disciplinary superstructure to keep the working class in it proper place, i.e. outside the ownership of capital. However, it is my contention that Hayek in his view has in mind a society, a human group, where culture is in formation. Because for Hayek everything – i.e. morals, reason, self-interested calculative thinking – is (a product of) culture, we cannot assume anything as given. Thus it is not possible to have individuals with calculative self-interested minds who are consciously imposing superstition for their own gain in the world which we are talking about here, i.e. the dawn of human culture.

However, it is clear that we must have a great tension here because once private property has arisen, self-interest also comes to rest on a stronger ground, thereby (at least) partly conflicting the Elsterian requirements for functionalism. Therefore functionalism in the Hayekian mould is of a somewhat impure kind.[40] However, it would be wrong to say that it fails Elster's 'test' because if we think of the immense scope – measured in time and culture – of the Hayekian functionalism this should come as no surprise. It would not, I think, be impossible to construct more specific cycles that would pass the test. I will not, however, try to do that here.

Anyhow, at the following stage – in our ideal-type explanation – in the evolution of human culture would be exemplified by a cycle where private property has a function in inducing self-interested behaviour. And the following stage after that would be represented by a cycle where self-interest is functional in creating the market, i.e. we are now at cycle 2. Thus we have the following developmental sequence:

Innate morality/primitive altruistic man ⇒ superstition ⇒ private property ⇒ self-interest ⇒ market ⇒ evolved morality/ modern rational man

In this vein the change of an 'instinctive', 'altruistic' society to a 'rational' and 'selfish' society may be explained by successive chains of behavioral patterns and institutions in which the unintended consequence (i.e. the order)

---

this problem in point (5) below.
[40]Cf. Douglas (1986, 33ff) for a defense of 'imperfect' functionalism.

becomes the 'explanation'[41]

The story could be generalized to other belief-systems, such as the role of religion in industrialization. The 'classic' case here would be the Weberian conception of 'Protestant ethics'.

However, even if a developed version of the scenario above would be satisfying to explain the rather surprising emergence of calculating behaviour from altruistic instincts it is far from satisfying when considering the order as a whole, i.e. the 'totality of culture'. Even if Hayek's turning upside-down of the self-interest postulate, (i.e. in assuming altruism to be 'the original position') makes his system quite more comfortable with the explanation of such things as charity, voting, etc. than the self-interest explanation, we still need parallel stories of other institutions and behaviour as well. However, I will not try develop the theme of cultural development further in this chapter.

For Hayek culture, in all its complexity, is to be understood in the same sense as the existence of market and self-interest above, i.e. as traits that are functional for the existence for the human race in its actual extension. Indeed, the maximal extension of the 'extended order' seems to be the only 'goal' which Hayek accepts for evolution.

To what has been said hitherto must immediately be added that it seems questionable whether Hayek would have accepted the above functional cycle of economizing behaviour and the market mechanism except as a pedagogical simplification. For Hayek man was neither especially selfish nor rational. 'Economizing behaviour' for him, following Menger, was an idealization of a process which was in reality a mixture of innovative activity and imitation. This idealizing feature holds, of course, for the proposed 'chain of functional cycles'. But perhaps Hayek would have accepted the functional explanations as a (specific) generalization of his system, or perhaps as describing a mechanism in his system. Still it should be kept in mind that one of the most remarkable features in Hayek's thought is that the reality in its entire complexity is uncomprehensible .

Verstehen and meaning once again

We have yet to say some words about *verstehen* which seems to give Hayek's functionalism its anthropological flavour. As mentioned earlier, the key to the Hayekian evolutionary process is group selection:[42]

---

[41]See also the first quotation in the next section about *verstehen*.

[42]Despite all this talk about selection, Hayek does not accept, rightly I think, title 'sociobiologist': *"Culture is neither natural nor artificial, neither genetically transmitted nor rationally designed"* (Hayek 1982c, 155).

This implies a sort of inversion of the relation between cause and effect in the sense that the structures possessing a kind of order will exist because the elements do what is necessary to secure the persistence of that order. The 'final cause' or 'purpose', i.e., the adaptation of the parts to the requirements of the whole, becomes a necessary part of the explanation of why structures of the kind exist: we are bound to explain the fact that the elements behave in a certain way by the circumstance that this sort of conduct is most likely to preserve the whole – on the preservation of which depends the preservation of the individuals, which would therefore not exist if they did not behave in this manner. A 'teleological' explanation is thus entirely in order so long as it does not imply design by a maker but merely the recognition that the kind of structure would not have perpetuated itself if it did not act in a manner likely to produce certain effects and that it has evolved through those prevailing at each stage who did. (Hayek 1967, 77)

This quotation makes clear that the central feature in a functional explanation, besides the biological metaphor, is the search for the meaning and purpose of different behavioral patterns, which means that it is a question of *verstehen.*

Now it may be claimed that such a theory of *verstehen* should not be needed for functional explanation. It could be considered as no more needed than a conception like 'wings want to fly' in a biological explanation of the function of wings. However, this is not Hayek's view. It would of course be possible to understand action also in physical terms or try to understand the society from outside, like an ant-heap,[43]

[b]ut if we tried to do so for the purposes of explaining human action, we would confine ourselves to less than we know about the situation. (Hayek 1942, 277)

Here we may tie the discussion to the earlier discussion about meaning. I think we can in the spirit of Hayek's general message distinguish between two types of 'meaning'. Firstly we have the scientific meaning which Hayek just named teleological and in which our understanding of the mechanisms as the invisible hand is very important. But there is an other kind of meaning

---

[43]See also Hayek's discussion of *verstehen*: "The theoretical social sciences [...] in their efforts to account for the unintended consequenses of individual actions, endeavour to reconstruct the individual reasoning from the data which to him are provided by the recognition of the actions of others as meaningful wholes (Hayek 1967, 58-60).

which has to do with the involvement and understanding of tradition at a common-sense level. This understanding, which may be called first order understanding (or meaning) I think is essential for the other type of meaning, which may be called second order understanding. I do not here want to claim that *verstehen* is indispensable for the understanding of invisible hand-mechanisms in general, but Hayek seems to put a great weight on it. The other feature is the role 'meaning' has in 'transmission' of culture, i.e. we do not understand the 'why' of culture but we understand its 'what'. Without this 'what', i.e. intelligibility of behaviour, there would not, at least according to Hayek's social philosophy, be any invisible hand of the market either.

Concluding remarks

As noted at the beginning of this chapter no attempt will be made to say the last word on Hayek. Of course only what little was introduced of Hayek's ideas here invites vast amount of questions. I will restrict my concluding comments to the relation between the proposed functionalism and some of the ethical views that are involved here concerning the importance of economic values in the role they appear to have in Hayek's social philosophy.

Firstly, the problem of design *contra* spontaneous order. There is in Hayek's works no distinction of what would be ('permissible') spontaneous change and what would be design in an impermissible degree. Because all cultural evolution is the result of human action and in that sense (of partial) individual 'design' on different levels, how great should this impact on the general system allowed to be? How abrupt are these changes allowed to be? It is difficult to interpret Hayek's view otherwise than that 'permissible design' must be 'atomistic' – somehow like a firm in perfect competition. It is understandable that Hayek has great problems with systems which do not have these characteristics, such as representative democracy. However, Hayek does not seem to be quite consequent on this point. Compare the following passage:

> Since our aim must be to discover what role particular institu-
> tions and traditions play in the functioning of society, we must
> constantly put the dissolving acid of reason to values and cus-
> toms which not only are dear to others but are also so largely the
> cement which keeps the society together. (Hayek 1967, 130)

with a later passage such as "No longer the end pursued but the rules ob-
served make the action good or bad" (Hayek 1988, 81). If this is the case we can no more be critical of the rules because we cannot understand the overall

consequences. We have no other choice, but to follow the rules. This also follows from the fact that the rules are largely unconscious. I will not pursue this theme further here, but it seems that Hayek in his latest work *Fatal Conceit* became more skeptical of the limits of reason than he was before.

Secondly, it seems as if Hayek sometimes forgets that competition itself may be seen as an evolutionary process which is *co-evolutive* in the same sense as natural evolution. This means – among other things – that the market is no longer 'inhabited by the same species' as in its beginning and is accordingly itself something different. We today appear to have species that have changed e.g in size and structure, which means that they probably also have changed in complexity. Briefly put, the 'tool-function' which Hayek invests in the market may have changed and its species may have 'wills of their own' that will differ from Hayek's theoretical conclusions.

Thirdly, and related to the second argument: As the market may have made us more industrious, polite etc., it may also be that this change of values changes with the economy. I.e., beside the useful market-mindedness it can also create the belief e.g. that such a view is enough for living in and maintaining the society. As Hayek himself repeatedly, although not perhaps always so explicitly, notes, 'market values' are not enough for keeping the society together.

Fourthly, what makes Hayek interesting and at the same time problematic, is that for him a question like 'do economic values destroy other values essential for the existence of society' does not exist within his system. Economic, moral, religious or whatever values exist because they are viable, or have survived, or rather that the bearers – i.e. the human groups – of these values have survived. So we are always living in a kind of 'best of possible worlds', when 'best' is defined in 'survival value'. What must be emphasized here, however, is that the rules for survival might be quite different in cultural evolution than natural evolution.

This brings us to a connected point of view which generally speaking is perhaps the greatest flaw in Hayek's system; he cannot, or refuses to see unintended consequences that are not beneficial. This is a problem which has been discussed within economics almost as long as it has existed under the term 'market failures'. However, because a considerable literature exists on these I will only make some comments of a more general character.

Why could not the invisible hand produce unintended effects which are not functional – in the long run, of course? Of course it is natural not to observe such dysfunctional traits or institutions, because they have disappeared in the evolutionary history. The problem with Hayekian view, 'the best of worlds', considered as a result of an evolutionary process, is that we do not know, considering from *status quo*, which function will prove to be a dysfunction *ex post*. Hayek is of course conscious of this. Indeed the gradualism which Hayek defends is based on the consideration of avoiding too big mistakes. The viability of the market system has now been 'tested' in a few hundred years against other systems like tradition, barter economy, feudalism and recently, socialism. Still, the conclusion of Hayek of the finality of the market order seems very bold indeed. It is not at all precluded that in the perspective of millennia that Hayek is looking, the market order will prove to be a monstrosity. Of course this may not change the main argument of Hayek; our present situation may not allow any creation by willing to do so superior to the market even in the long run. Evolution may create other behavioral patterns and institutions in the future, but given the ones we have this is the best of possible worlds?

3 Absolute values, work and consumption – some conceptual remarks

Tage Kurtén

In this article I will investigate a certain way of evaluating two central elements in economic life, *work* and *consumption*. I will start with a view, articulated in an interview-based study concerning life-views, where work is viewed as something very important in man's life, while consumption is seen as something quite superficial and empty.

How are we to understand the expressions of these attitudes? I will suggest that the concept *absolute value* helps us in our understanding. This concept is, however, viewed with suspicion by many philosophers today. This is pointed out by Roy F. Holland for example (see Holland (1980), 126-127). My argument is that we in certain situations do take an attitude towards certain features in life presupposing something absolute. I will point to some ambiguities in our manner of using the concept of absolute values. For example there seem to be two different ways in which we talk meaningfully about something absolute, one moral and one non-moral. I will also point to the close connection between talking about absolute values and the language of religion.

A way of speaking of work and consumption

When asked about the meaning of life, AA, a female writer, born in the 50's, stresses physically tangible events, such as human work or the experience of giving birth to a child. She deems these phenomena extremely important and states for example the following about work:

> I think it's a basic insight, [...] how important work is for us
> human beings. [...] that a man does his job and deems his job
> valuable, that he is proud of doing this job. What an important
> [life]content a man has when he is able to say, 'I have done my
> job as well as I have been able to', and how this gives him a sort
> of stature and dignity. (Interview 30.8.1988, 9.)[1]

The interview was done in 1988. In a later interview, conducted in 1992,
when the economic situation in Finland had radically changed resulting in an
unprecedented high rate of unemployment, she stressed even more emphat-
ically the importance of work, and the disastrous consequences of becoming
unemployed.

> Work has generally such a value [...] that it is horrible in my
> opinion and the most cruel thing, when meaningful work is taken
> away from people. Or that a person right from the start is refused
> the right to a meaningful job, which could give him satisfaction.
> (Interview 9.12.1992, 22)

The interviewer asks AA what she thinks about survival strategies for the
unemployed, and she answers:

> What is needed in this situation is a very strong spirit. Around me
> here in my local community there are also unemployed people. All
> kinds of factories where people have worked have been shut down.
> So there has been a terrible number of suicides. I have seen how
> people in a short period of time, in a few months, have become
> alcoholics in the pubs. [...] It is extremely important for one's self-
> esteem that a person feels that he in a way meaningfully redeems
> his existence and that he produces some form of positive profit
> for the world. [...] Man will easily become mentally bankrupt,
> if he doesn't manage to find some strategy for survival, some
> meaningful content in life. (Interview 9.12.1992, 23)

AA is at the same time very critical of the consumption traits she wit-
nesses in modern Finnish society. She thinks the lifestyle of many Finns is
very superficial.

---

[1]The interview belongs to a larger interview-based study. About fifty Finnish writers
have been interviewed concerning their life-views. I have translated the quotations freely
from Finnish. References are made to the transcribed version of the taped interviews
(Kurtén 1993).

Man has been given some 60 – 70 years here and he uses this time in the following way: From birth, he is sucked into a pipe; he goes to school, and in school he is taught some basic skills and so he gets on in some profession and starts to work without any more passion or interest of his own in order to get money to be able to buy anything that is offered and everything that he according to magazines and advertisements and competition is supposed to acquire. Then when he has obtained enough and got married and had children and dies, although he now has done what people over the centuries have been doing [...] there is somehow something on a very low level mentally in all this. [...] I think a person has been alive in a more concrete sense, when he has fought or suffered or something like that for the sake of something.

Interviewer: Do you mean that man also acquires more human dignity when he lives...?

Yes indeed. [—] I don't think that buying things – which nowa-days is a hobby for people, you cannot deny that – it does not give you as much as it promises. You desire a beautiful set of sheets which you can buy with a coupon and you go and buy it. I think that you all the same after doing that rather have a feeling of emptiness. But then, when you have given birth to a child and experienced all the pain, then you think that I have put up with all this. As a person, living fully, I have experienced this. Then there is no empty feeling, even after the child is born. The feeling is complete and intense. (Interview 30.8.1993, 19-20)

These thoughts of AA are perhaps not very unique. The question is, however, how we are to understand them. What does a high valuation of work really mean? And how could the superficiality of a consumistic lifestyle be understood? Do we here see only examples of AA's subjective opinions or can we consider a wider objectivity in the way values are actualized?

Before going further into that, it is in its place to define somehow the concepts of 'work' and 'consumption'. It is quite obvious that both concepts are used in different ways in a number of different contexts. To work is, primarily, to be productive in some sense. To consume is in a way the opposite, something unproductive. Work can be done in order to attain results, the things produced (which also includes getting things done in social contexts, like decision- making on the board of a company and so on). The things produced can be of vital importance for one's own life, like fishing for a fisherman. Things can be produced for the needs of our fellow human beings. But work can also be done for the income, the money that is needed in order for someone to live and to consume goods. By means of work one can take part in all kinds of undertakings, morally deficient as well as morally good ones. The value of work has, of course, something to do with all these aspects. Our reflections concern work in all these senses. Primarily I will discuss the kind of activity that we in an everyday Western life call 'work' in the sense of "going to work", "being employed", "having a job", "keeping the household going" and so forth.[2]

Also 'consumption' can have a great variety of meanings. In order to live we all must consume. Only by so doing can we satisfy some of our basic natural needs. In more "primitive" cultures, the borderline between work and consumption is not very clear – think again of a culture of fishermen. Consumption on this life-sustaining level does not concern us here. What AA in the quotation seems to be referring to is a kind of consumption, which goes far beyond the satisfying of basic needs. It is what is sometimes called *'consumism'*.[3] I intend to discuss the kind of values which are coming here to the fore. There are many aspects of consumption which we will not probe here. The borderline between necessary and luxurious consumption is for example indefinite and partly intertwined with culture. This is, of course, part of our problem. I, however, think that we can meaningfully discuss problems concerning "luxurious consumption" and the role it can play in

[2]The Finnish sociologist, Matti Kortteinen has studied the culture of work among employees in Finnish mechanical industries and bank-offices in his dissertation, *Kunnian kenttä* (The Field of Honour). Among other things he finds a feature with ethical dimensions: the individual is ready to sacrifice himself in order to do his job. This is a question of honour to him. The narratives given by different employees speak of hardships and the ability to endure them. They do not speak of aims outside of work; only of surviving through work, which for the male workers is a very individualistic matter. In engineering workshops honour is a question of tackling successfully every challenge in work as an individual. For female clerks in Finnish banks, the view is more social than individualistic. There honour is more a question of doing one's part in a team effort, and the moral requirements concern their way of taking their due place on the team. (Cf. Kortteinen (1992), 60-62; 67-72.)

[3]The Swedish sociologist, Gunnar Adler-Karlsson, has for example also pointed to the importance that obtaining material goods seems to have in people's lives. (Cf. Adler-Karlsson (1990), 240-243.) In an earlier book Adler-Karlsson was very critical of a consumistic lifestyle. In his more recent book he is more understanding of it, mainly because he thinks that maintaining the world economy presupposes a consumistic behaviour. He therefore advocates a lighter form of consumism, although he is still critical of materialistically oriented consumption. (Cf. Adler-KarlssonAdler-Karlsson (1977), 16, 133-136; 1990, 307-309, 302-303.) From a more ethnological viewpoint, Orvar Löfgren has stressed the importance of material things in people's life-narratives. The acquisition of commodities has an important symbolic role in people's lives, he has found. "This was the year when my Daddy bought our first Volvo." This points to an important integrative role that some sort of consumptive behaviour has in many westerners' lives. Cf. Löfgren (1992, 269-287).

people's lives, without going into a far-reaching discussion of where to draw the line.

Internal and external values

When considering AA's high valuation of work, could we understand it by pointing at something outside work? Could it lie in some other value, in the pursuit of which work is done? Classical utilitarianism, for example, viewed happiness as being the only goal worth striving for. Here we touch upon a distinction between internal and external values, which Alasdair MacIntyre has discussed in an illuminating way.

If, for example, happiness were the only value worth striving for, work could not be of value in itself. It would then be of value only as long as it could contribute to man's happiness.[4] Is it at all possible to understand the value of work as anything more than a means to some more important end (value)? I think there are good reasons to claim that it is possible, although some moral philosophers seem to deny this. (Cf. for example Grenholm (1993, 295) and note 17 below.)

When trying to explain what he means by a virtue, Alasdair MacIntyre defines a notion of 'practice' for which a distinction between *internal* and *external goods* is crucial. For my purpose here I am only interested in this distinction – we don't have to discuss the adequacy of MacIntyre's theory of virtues.[5]

MacIntyre takes the example of a boy whom he wishes to teach to play chess. The child has no interest in chess but indeed in candies. By offering him fifty cents worth of candy when playing, and even more candy when winning a game, he manages to get the boy to play and to try his best. The point is, that as long as he plays to get the candy, the boy is only striving for external goods. He has then no good reason for example not to cheat, provided he can do so successfully. But there is something more to playing chess, MacIntyre states:

> But, so we may hope, there will come a time when the child
> will find in those goods specific to chess, in the achievement of a
> certain highly particular kind of analytical skill, strategic imag-

---

[4]This is sometimes the way people do relate to their jobs. See, for example, Grenholm (1988, 70, 72-76).

[5]Gaita has, for example, criticized MacIntyre's way of treating the virtue of fidelity for making it into something only functionally valuable. Thereby MacIntyre misses the valuation of fidelity for its own sake. See Gaita (1991, 84-85).

ination and competitive intensity, a new set of reasons, reasons
now not just for winning on a particular occasion, but for trying
to excel in whatever way the game of chess demands. Now if
the child cheats, he or she will be defeating not me, but himself.
(MacIntyre 1990, 188)

There are in chessplaying *internal goods* which cannot be achieved as long
as the aim is the external values. These internal goods have to do with the
acting subject himself.

If we apply this point to the phenomena we are discussing, what do we
see? The concept of internal good could be applied to AA's way of talking
about work. Saying that there is something internally good in doing one's
job would be to say that in the activity of working it is possible to experience
a value, which you fail to see and grasp if you completely take your job as
a means to some external goods, like money or happiness. We could then
interpret AA's way of describing how "proud" one is of doing one's job, how
important a life value man's doing his job well is to him, how terrible a thing
you do to a person when you take his job away from him, and how important
for the self-esteem it is for man to find he redeems his existence through
work, etc., as examples of just this kind of internal value. For example,
"self-esteem" should then not be taken as a psychological value, external to
the activity, but as a way of expressing the internal interplay of giving and
taking – hardships and feelings of deep satisfaction – which doing one's job,
and doing it well is about. In this perspective the problem with a man who
is not doing his job well, is not *primarily* that he is cheating his employer or
a future consumer of the things he produces, but that he is cheating himself.

This value, internal to the activity, seems to be very fragile, sensitive to
all sorts of external factors. The concept of internal value seems to shed
some light upon the fact that this element of work will be corrupted when
an employer tries to use this feeling of value by the worker for his own ends.
One could ask if it is possible for the employer to talk about this element
of internal value in work without it being corrupted and transformed into
something external?

In light of such internal values it is perhaps also easier to see why every
kind of work does not seem to enjoy the same status. The purpose of the
working process may change the possibility to see an internal value in one's
work. Think for example of an industry producing knick-knackery, or nuclear
weapons. The possibility of experiencing an internal value in doing one's job
well in such production is different from the value of work for example to a
nurse, or to a worker in a medical factory.

MacIntyre's story helps us also to understand the disastrous effects that an economy and a society which only stress external goods in relation to work can have on a person. When we think of a milieu, where the work is done only for the sake of the money which enables one to buy new things, as in AA's critical story, we find an example of what it is like to be unable to see anything internally good in work.

Absolute and relative values

I think that the quotations above illustrate something further about our way of relating to phenomena like work and consumption. It has to do with seeing some phenomenon in life as having an absolute value in some sense. An absolute value is somehow connected to an internal value, but the concepts are also clearly different.

In what sense do we talk about values as absolute? I find Ludwig Wittgenstein's treatment of this question in his lecture on ethics illuminating. He is there primarily interested in an absolute *moral* value. He considers a distinction between absolute and relative values, relating our morality to something absolute. He explains what he means by means of an example:

Think of a man who plays tennis and you say to him: "You play tennis pretty badly." If the other then answers: "Yes I know, but I don't want to play any better", you could leave it at that. Then think of a man telling a complete lie and you said to him "You are behaving quite awfully." If he then answered, "I know I behaved badly, but I don't want to behave any better" could you then respond, "Well all right, that's your business"? Wittgenstein's point here is that this is not possible. Instead the natural reaction would be something like "You ought to want to behave better!". (Cf. Wittgenstein (1965, 5).) What Wittgenstein wants to point out by this is a judgement of absolute value.[6]

He contrasts these kinds of absolute values with "trivial" or "relative" values. A relative value is at stake when we for instance speak of a good chair: "This means that the chair serves a certain predetermined purpose and the word good here has only meaning as far as this purpose has been previously fixed upon." (Wittgenstein 1965, 5)

If we accept Wittgenstein's point, in what sense could this distinction relate to the concepts of work and consumption which our introductory interview texts described?

I think we can understand AA's manner of speaking of work as indicative of something absolute in some sense. In a man's relation to his work there

---

[6]For a similar point, see also Gaita (1991, 198-200); Taylor (1989, 20-21).

can obviously be this absolute valuation of a moral kind. That comes to fore
for example when AA speaks of how a man is proud of doing his job and
doing it well, how this gives him a sense of dignity and so on. Here we have
this moral feature which would cause us to morally blame a man who says:
"I know I do my job badly, but I don't want to do it any better."

When we think of AA's image of a consumistic lifestyle, it is quite obvious
that she does not find any absolute value in that. According to AA's view,
consumism should be taken as pursuing only relative values. Finding morally
absolute values in following the demands of the consumer society ("always
following the latest fashion", "evaluating fellow-citizens according to their
level of consumption", etc.) would be strange. (Remember here that we are
not considering basic, life-sustaining consumption.) Wittgenstein's concept
has helped us a step forward. But what exactly have we found?

A statement of fact?

Talking about internal and absolute values, in connection with for example
work, expresses different but related ways of understanding work. An absolute value can sometimes not be understood, if one does not see any internal
value. For example, when work is done only for the salary, when one finds
no internal value in work, one misses the possibility of being proud of one's
job, of feeling a sense of dignity in doing one's job well, and so on. One
cannot understand the moral claims inherent in the activity. But, on the
other hand, there seem to be situations where the absolute value does not
have to be internal, for example when work is done for the sake of others.
The farmer cultivating his land in a situation of scarcity of food, can feel an
absolute demand to do his best, because of values external to the working
process itself.

Not every internal good has, on the other hand, to be of an absolute
nature. Think of Wittgenstein's example of the tennis-player. In playing
tennis there are some values totally internal to the activity, achievable only
when you play tennis for its own sake, and not for something external. Think
of the contrast between the girl who whole-heartedly wants to play a game
of tennis with a boy, and the boy who only plays in order to get to know
the girl better – the possibility that he will be a disappointment to her is
quite obvious. He does not play for the sake of the game itself. Nevertheless
we would hesitate to speak of the girl's attitude to tennis as taking this to
be something absolute.[7] On the other hand, however, we would very well

---

[7]Even sports can, of course, turn into something absolute, into "a matter of life and

understand the girl if she blamed (morally) the boy for not taking the game seriously. Is this a reason to see playing tennis as an absolute moral value for the girl? I do not think so. Her blame would primarily concern the attitude of the boy towards the whole situation – not only the concrete game of tennis.

What then does it mean to say that something, such as work, has an absolute character? Is it a quality of the work in itself? If so, then it could be a statement of fact, that work has this quality. (See Wittgenstein (1965, 6).) But is that possible? Wittgenstein argues that only relative values can be the object of statements of fact. If so, then it is impossible to capture "the absoluteness" so to say in adequate terms, by referring to something empirical. The only way of actualizing something absolute in value, is then by giving examples of life-situations in which you think it is adequate to speak of something absolute. (Cf. Wittgenstein (1965, 7-8).)

> Now let us see what we could possibly mean by the expression, "*the* absolutely right road." I think it would be the road which *everybody* on seeing it would, *with logical necessity*, have to go, or be ashamed for not going. And similarly the *absolutely good*, if it is a describable state of affairs, would be one which everybody, independent of his tastes and inclinations, would *necessarily* bring about or feel guilty for not bringing about. And I want to say that such a state of affairs is a chimera. No state of affairs has, in itself, what I would like to call the coercive power of an absolute judge. Then what have all of us who, like myself, are still tempted to use such expressions as 'absolute good', 'absolute value', etc., what have we in mind and what do we try to express? Now whenever I try to make this clear to myself it is natural that I should recall cases in which I would certainly use these expressions [...]. (Wittgenstein 1965, 7)

We could then ask if this has made us any wiser. My intention was to look at the introductory text in the light of the concept of absolute value. But what we have is merely an invitation to look at the utterances we started with. There is no definition of 'the absolute' which could be used as a standard for judging if AA is describing something absolute, when she is talking about work. (The same goes for "internal value".) Perhaps it would suffice to mention the concept of something absolute (and internal).[8] Thereby *our*

---

death", which can be seen in sports on an elite level, and in all the repercussions professional sports have in the life of talented young boys and girls. In Finland this can be seen especially in ice-hockey.

[8]That something has an absolute value to us could of course be expressed in different words, like "very important", "a matter of life and death" and so on.

attention is directed to the phenomenon discussed in a different way.[9] If we then consider something absolute in the phenomenon, this does not have to mean a special quality of the phenomenon itself. It has more to do with our own responses to the phenomenon in question.

Some ambiguities of absoluteness

Another way of discerning the absoluteness of a value, is to look for different ways in which the concept of absolute value is used.

Our interview text also points to a danger, which the idea of an absolute value seems to embrace. There is something ambivalent in the way taking something as an absolute can function in a person's life. This can be seen in AA's observations regarding work. She demonstrates how losing one's job also could mean losing one's sense of the meaning of life. The report about the suicides, which AA wants to explain with the deep value lost in becoming unemployed, provides an example of how some historical fact, the fact that you have or you don't have a job, is taken to have such an ultimate value, that becoming unemployed takes the whole purpose of living away.

If we look at what Wittgenstein says, I think we find that he would not regard this as an example of an absolute value in a *moral* sense. Already in the quotation of Wittgenstein we saw that he did not want to equate the absolute with anything empirical or historically given: "No state of affairs has, in itself, what I would like to call the coercive power of an absolute judge."

If we accept this, then we have a two-fold understanding of absolute values, one of a *moral* and one of a *non-moral* kind. I think the concept of "basic trust"[10] facilitates the understanding of this distinction. Man's basic trust concerns ultimate values in his life. In some sense basic trust has to do with what a man deems most important in life, that which makes life worth living. It has to do with a basic level of meaning in life. By definition it is hard for a man when he is shaken in his basic trust. If the foundation of his life is taken away from him, despair cannot be far off.

AA's talk of the hopeless situation of people becoming unemployed could be understood in this light. When work is taken as an absolute value in this sense, then losing one's job can lead one to despair. The absolute value in this sense does not have to be of a moral kind. The difference in grammar

---

[9]Holland for example hints at such a solution. (See Holland (1980, 128).)

[10]In another context I have discussed that concept in greater depth, in relation to central elements in people's lifeviews. (Cf. Kurtén (1992).)

between these two kinds of discourses could be expressed as the difference between *taking something as* an absolute value, and *realizing that* something is of an absolute value.

The distinction between a moral and a non-moral understanding of an absolute value helps us to grasp some other aspects of the concept of an absolute value.

It is quite obvious that a man's sense of absolute values can change over his lifetime. By his own way of acting a man can demonstrate that something has changed from being of absolute value to him into something relative. You could think of a professor who starts his career by committing himself to his research and his teaching. As time goes by he becomes more and more cynical and loses his belief in what he is doing. He keeps his professorship, but tries to do as little as possible and finds pleasure only in leisure activities. Others could then blame him (morally) for what he has become. His loss of an absolute value would be the reason for that blame. He has not stuck to a profound moral value concerning work.

But when the circumstances change, sticking to an absolute value can cause destruction and therefore cause others to blame the person morally. This could be seen from the example of unemployment. Here it is important to recall the distinction between two ways of relating to an absolute value. If we do not realize this, there is a danger that the phenomenon, which had an internal, constructive point in a particular activity and a particular situation, turns into something destructive, when the absoluteness is attached to it regardless of the context. Sticking to a value (work as the meaning of life) in a non-moral sense could lead to a morally disastrous situation. Finding an absolute value in work in one situation does not guarantee that this absoluteness of work remains in every new situation. This is, of course, only another way of saying that elements in life only make sense in their specific contexts.

But does this not contradict a central point in our treatment of absoluteness? We could think of another remark by Wittgenstein. In his lectures on religion he gives the example of a writer (obviously Søren Kierkegaard) who as a boy had got a task from his father. He had suddenly felt that nothing, not even death, could take away the responsibility for the task. The writer saw this as a form of proof of the immortality of the soul. Wittgenstein seems to agree with Kierkegaard's main point here. That implies that he at least finds the idea of an absolute duty, which not even death can overcome, intelligible. If we accept this, does it mean that the idea of something absolute here is about something morally valid regardless of time and space? I would say yes, in a way. But not in such a way that we contradict what we earlier stated about the possibility of circumstances changing so much that something loses its moral value.

In this connection we could consider a working culture like that described by Matti Kortteinen (and which also seems to be presupposed by AA).[11] Kortteinen describes a culture, where the absoluteness of work is manifested in an internal demand on every participant to live up to the picture of a man managing everything by himself. This means a culture which easily becomes very judgemental of everyone who fails: a culture which erects walls against those outside.[12] When work is taken as something absolute in this way some destructive elements seem to lie hidden in it. It leads to a practical morality where you honour those who belong to the same group and those who manage in the hardships of work. But it seems to have no place for those outside, and for the weak ones, who cannot live up to the demands work places.[13] An interesting question, which I do not intend to answer, is if work here is seen as an absolute value in a moral or a non-moral sense. The simple fact that an undertaking does have destructive features, does not imply that there could not be a moral striving by the participants. A terrifying example is Rudolph Höss, the commandant of Auschwitz, who is said to have regarded his job as an absolute moral duty.

I hope my argument has convinced my reader that there is a meaningful use of the concept of an absolute value in connection to work, and that an absolute value can be seen as both moral and non-moral. The point of an absolute value lies in the way the individual responds to the demands of life. That means that speaking of an absolute value loses much of its point, if the absoluteness is dictated by someone else. The moral point can be missed, if the individual is judged entirely from another person's perspective. I do not think that the fact that you could be blamed for not living up to some value[14] is in conflict with this. The point of blame lies in your accepting it or failing to view it as valid. In the last resort the individual is himself his own judge.

---

[11]See above note 2.

[12]Kortteinen for example describes how he had to show off, in order to be accepted by the workers he was studying. (Cf. Kortteinen (1992, 98-103).) But this can, of course, also be seen as a way of testing if Kortteinen was taking the interviewees seriously.

[13]Perhaps it is something like this which Holland, in line with Plato's famous parable, calls "the absolutism of the cave". (Cf. Holland (1980, 129).)

[14]Cf. Wittgenstein's example above of the man who was lying.

Absolute values and religious language

The borderline between a moral and a non-moral mode of understanding an absolute value is not always very clear. Perhaps we could take them as two aspects of the same thing. We could think of an idealistic philosophy of life, where the absolute Good is the object of basic trust and in the light of which all moral judgements are made. Holland writes about the "absolutism of the cave" in an attempt to describe the moral dilemma of modern man. (Cf. Holland (1980, 128-130).) According to him Plato, with his famous parable of the cave, manages to point out that man is always in danger of absolutizing the shadows of the cave instead of letting the ideal world shed its judging light on man's life. The dilemma of our secular culture is in the light of this that many people have lost their sense of the ideally good. A religious language can be understood as an attempt, with a long tradition, to tackle precisely this kind of dilemma. I will therefore point to some features in religious language, which also struggle with these very questions.

Absolute values taken as above resemble a religious way of talking about and relating to some phenomena in life. If we think of an attitude towards work which is often attached to Lutheranism we find traits which resemble the ambigious role absolute values play in the above discussion.

In a recent work Carl-Henric Grenholm has studied what he calls "protestant work ethics". In it he provides a presentation of a Lutheran doctrine of vocation.[15]

A Christian view in accordance with Lutheran thinking evaluates work from two vantage points. Firstly, work is seen as an instrument of God's continuous act of creation. Through human work God gives human beings what they require to live a tolerable life and this serves to make work very important. The value of work is understood in the light of God the creator who sustains the world and human life. Work is seen "sub specie aeternitatis". Secondly, work is valued because our fellow human beings are thereby served. Through our work our neighbour is offered something good.[16] We could say that the former point, where work is valued as part of God's ongoing creative activity, comes close to what we earlier understood as an internal absolute value in work. The second point, where the service of others is stressed, exemplifies an absolute demand of something external in relation to work.

---

[15]This can be of interest to our investigation because Martin Luther historically represented a much greater appreciation of human manual labour than earlier, important western thinkers such as for example the ancient Greek philosophers and the central medieval thinker Thomas Aquinas. (Cf. Grenholm (1993, 37-41).)

[16]Cf. Grenholm (1993, 46-47); Grenholm (1988, 402-403). See also his own formulation of a Christian view of work in modern times, Grenholm (1993, 296).

Although the example is taken from a Lutheran tradition, the point I am trying to make concerns religious talk of God in connection with worldly activities more generally. Such religious language can be seen as another way of explicating the difficulty of attributing something quite ordinary a value which is not relative, without implying that the phenomenon thus valued is placed above every natural human context. Religious language could thereby express a way of understanding the absolute value of, for example, work without losing sight of a sense in which the value of work is relative, because everything in the last resort rests in God.[17] This is a major point in talking of one's work as a vocation.

The difference between an absolute value in a moral and a non-moral sense comes in this religious perspective to the fore when God is taken as the object of basic trust (the point of faith). Although work on the human level can still be regarded as a morally absolute value, the inclination to make work an absolute value also in a non-moral sense seems to be lacking. The space for an absolute value in this sense is already occupied by God, the creator. A religious mode of talking about work can thus be understood (seen) as an expression of a general human dilemma concerning our ability to put our most profound valuations into words. This indicates how the borderline between what we would call moral and religious language is not very clear. The vague borderline between moral values and religious expressions is also illustrated by Wittgenstein in his above mentioned lecture on ethics. (Cf. Wittgenstein (1965, 8-11).) A more recent example can be found in Raimond Gaita's work on absolute values. (Cf. Gaita (1991, 218-225).) Perhaps this could help us understand why many people in the modern world seem to have forgotten the possibility of taking some values as absolute at the same time as they have lost sight of the meaningfulness of religious language and of a religious way of life.

---

[17]In a sense I think in his way of treating work, Grenholm does not quite manage to grasp this point. That becomes clear when he says: "What value then has work in relation to other human activities? The answer to this question depends on the aims which are realizable through our work. Human work is not namely an end in itself which is valuable independently of its potential use. In this sense, it does not have an intrinsic value." (Grenholm 1993, 295) I think Grenholm in this quotation fails to see a distinction which, I hope, has become clear through my analysis. In the light of this it is possible to find an internal value in work, without necessarily excluding that work at the same time can be said to be dependent on the potential use of its results.

Consumption and absolute judgements

In the quotations with which this article started, AA also pointed to what we could call a consumistic lifestyle. She is herself very critical of it, but seems to presuppose that this way of living is quite common.[18] This view of life also stresses an instrumental view of work, whereby work is hardly ever seen as valuable in its own right. A materialistic, commodity-oriented lifestyle seems sometimes to express an absolute evaluation of a consumistic attitude towards life.[19] The Catholic philosopher John F. Kavanaugh is quite explicit on this point. He talks of "the commodity form" which he understands as a world-view. Such a world-view seems to represent something absolute in the life of the person who embraces it:

> The Commodity Form is in many ways a 'worldview'. [...] We could compare it to tinted glasses, which filter all seen objects in a prejudiced way. But the 'filter' in our case is not merely visual. The Commodity Form filters all our experiences, our attitudes and feelings, our emotions and drives, our perceptions, our behavior. [...] The content of the Commodity Form is marketing, producing, and consuming; and its result is a revelation of ourselves as replaceable objects whose goal and value is dependent upon how much we market, produce, and consume. [—] Possessions which might otherwise serve as expressions of our humanity, and enhance us as persons, are transformed into ultimates. Our being is in having. Our happiness is said to be in possessing more. Our drive to consume, bolstered by an economics of infinite growth, becomes addictive: it moves from manipulated need, to the promise of joy in things, to broken promises and frustrated expectation, to guilt and greater need for buying. Property is no longer instrumental to our lives; it is the final judge of our merit. (Kavanaugh 1989, 41-43)

According to Kavanaugh, the pre-eminent values in the "commodity form" are marketability and consumption. They serve as absolute values, conditioning our perception of value and importance. Thus they affect our self-understanding as well as our way of understanding the behavior of others.

---

[18]Most of us would probably intuitively agree. The view also receives support from sociological findings. See, for example, Grenholm's overview concerning Sweden (Grenholm 1988, 64-72). For the leading industrial country, the United States, see, for example, Bellah and Madsen (1992, 90-95).

[19]In a sense the point of Adler-Karlsson above (see note 3) hints at such an interpretation.

(Cf. Kavanaugh (1989, 21).) Here we are not interested in the accuracy of Kavanaugh's sketchy picture of modern-day culture. The important thing is to see what it could mean that this description was in some sense valid for a trait in an industrial culture, a trait whereby your success in the competition with others determines your value as a human being.

> The person *is* only insofar as he or she is marketable or productive. Human products, which should be valued only insofar as they enhance and express human worth, become the very standards against which human worth itself is measured. If our life's meaning is dictated by mercantilism and production, then our purpose and value are defined essentially in relation to what we can buy, what we can sell, or – at the very least – what we can hold on to. (Kavanaugh 1989, 22)

This, though not a very original nor new insight, is nevertheless important to our investigation, because it indicates a situation in which some basic features of the consumer and achievement-oriented market economy have attained the position of an absolute value.[20] In light of our discussion above, it seems obvious that the absolute value given to consumism is primarily of the non-moral kind. The phenomenon under discussion here is a human life in which some profound traits of the consumer society have the status of the most important position in life.

Implicit in AA's critical remarks about the emptiness of a consumism so described there is the distinction between moral and non-moral absolute values. AA expresses a moral judgement of a certain way of life.

In connection with this I will treat a discussion by Dewi Z. Phillips who offers an example of how a moral absolute judgement can be aimed also at oneself.

Phillips discusses Leo Tolstoy's short story *The Death of Ivan Ilych*. Phillips's main point is that Ilych never found anything wrong with his whole way of living during his active life (he had led a career-oriented life centered totally around the opportunities of furthering his own career (Cf. Dilman and Phillips (1971, 15-17)). When he was dying he changed his perspective on life totally. In that new perspective, what had previously felt most important, now seemed totally empty. He had found a way of understanding his life as a human being, which made his earlier life seem quite superficial to him. In the light of the meaning of life he came to see in the last moments

---

[20]Kavanaugh tells the story of Amy, a girl of fifteen who committed suicide, when she got her first B on her report card – hitherto all numbers had been A's. "If I fail in what I do, I fail in what I am", Amy wrote in her suicide note (Kavanaugh 1989, 21).

of his life, most of his earlier life seemed without meaning. (Cf. Dilman and Phillips (1971, 58-62).)

Phillips sees this new perspective as an absolute judgement. He suggests that the absolute judgement can be seen as a totally new aspect of life – an aspect that does not necessarily presuppose any awareness of the absoluteness of these values in life hitherto. There is at the same time a certain objective claim in this judgement, according to him – the judgement is valid regardless of how the person himself has understood his life.[21]

One point Phillips's analysis makes is that there can be a difference between taking some features of life (such as personal career, the possibility to work etc.) as absolute values, and the absoluteness of a moral value. It is the possibility to draw this distinction which makes it morally possible to judge ultimate values of others, or one's own former life. His account is an argument for our distinction between talking about absolute values in a moral and a non-moral sense.

Another point applied to our discussion could be that a consumistic lifestyle, though regarded as something absolutely valid and valuable by persons living according to it, could be regarded as morally blame-worthy because of the kind of lifestyle it is, in the light of another, deeper, perspective. Someone who accepts an absolute judgement, thinks it is valid, not because he accepts it, but because of the nature of the judgement.

This seems to contradict what I earlier stated about absolute values having a point only when a person recognizes it in him or herself. A contradiction is, however, not necessary. Phillips points to a danger in the way we have stated the matter, the danger of making moral judgements into something quite subjective. My point was that a judgement does not matter to the actor as long as he does not recognize the judgement as valid. The coming to see the judgement as valid is, however, not the same as coming to recognize an obvious fact. It is a question of judging one's own life from a certain perspective. As long as you do not have this view-point you do not see the point in question.

A third point which Phillips's text focuses on is the question of what kind of life a person leads. If we think of work and consumption in relation to this, they can both be seen as part of a person's life and giving a certain quality to the person's life. This quality could in one sense be deemed relative and subjective, but in another sense it has an objectivity and absoluteness, which the individual cannot escape. A major point in the absolute value of life seems to be that it is a *human* life. The absoluteness of traits in a

---

[21]See also Ilham Dilman's in one sense opposing view on this point (Dilman and Phillips 1971, 20-22).

person's life has to do with the absolute value of human dignity and of a human life as such.[22]

If we recall our discussion of work, the point that we are trying to make here is not that we hold this value of human life which gives value to work. It is in the absolute value of work that the value of human life takes expression under certain circumstances – internal to work is the point of human dignity and worth. This underlines the important interplay between the human subject, the things evaluated by that subject and the kind of life this subject leads.

Consumption and a religious view

We shall now briefly look at how the Catholic *theologian* Kavanaugh relates these phenomena to a religious language. What religious concepts does he use when he speaks of a consumer society? He claims that in a culture where the commodity form is dominant, human faith, human hope and human love, and also human freedom become impossible. He speaks here of *idolatry*. (Cf. Kavanaugh (1989, 44-45).) Idolatry is in this case to take commodities as ultimate values.

> True moral conflicts arise, however, when, in our well-founded and sane recognition that things, production, consumption, technical reason, even competition, cannot and should not be ignored in the building of human life, we accept these values as ultimates. (Kavanaugh 1989, 111-112)

He thus speaks of consumism as an absolute value – but he uses the expression in negative terms. Religiously, idolatry is a basic evil.[23] The problem that we met in the former part of this article, that of expressing an absolute value without absolutizing some historical and therefore relative fact, is a central problem even for Kavanaugh. When he relates his Christian faith to the specific cultural context he has described, he finds an important critical potential in faith:

> If only we Christians might realize the heights to which we are called by our incarnate, covenantal God. If only we might remember the utter newness and brilliance of what our faith implies. No

---

[22]This seems to be a logical truth, embedded in what we mean by a human being. If so, then a perspective where this is expressed also represents a certain objectivity.

[23]Idolatry is sometimes defined as the making of something conditional into something unconditional. Cf. Tillich (1951, 133,216); Tillich (1963, 355).

longer would we have to search for some identity, some justification in the garbage heap of commodities. No longer would we
clamor for some new savior or seducer. No longer would we even
conceive of a fake choice between seeking heaven and building the
earth. (Kavanaugh 1989, 153)

The point in the quotation seems to be that heaven is to be found while
building the earth. What is needed, according to him, is some kind of saint-
liness which is to be found *in* the world, not in any form of quietism.

A man or woman who lets the imperative to be human take its
deepest hold on his or her being, who becomes wholeheartedly
committed to the service of people and a world of justice, who
lives as he or she would call others to live – is nothing other than
a saint. (Kavanaugh 1989, 154)

Kavanaugh here combines the religious talk of God and a truly human
life in a way in which idolatry seems to be avoided. The saint reveals God,
but is himself convinced of the relativity of his own perfection:

Authentic sanctity [...] is discovered, finally, when human life
is seen as so splendid and irreplaceable a value that our very
God might become one with it. Men and women are of ines-
timable worth [...] because in the compassionate embrace of their
own truth, in the poverty of their being frighteningly incomplete,
they find themselves – vulnerable, yes, but radically opened in
freedom to the Fullness of personal knowing and loving. They
make incarnate their very God. (Kavanaugh 1989, 156)

The absoluteness that is indicated here, is the absolute value of human
life. It is it that gives value to human efforts in manual labour, because work
sustains human life, and it is an expression of human dignity. The same
principle of the absolute value of every human being seems to be the reason
why a consumistic lifestyle can never in itself be of absolute value. Such a
lifestyle seems to make a commodity even of the human being. We could ask,
finally, if such a recognition of the absolute value of every human life found
here in a religious discourse, and hinted at by Phillips in his deliberations,
could not shed some light on the deep valuation of work and the criticism
of consumption in the opening quotation of this article. This absolute value
of human life then seems to unite a religious and a more secular outlook on
life, and points in a similar direction concerning the value of work and of
consumption.[24]

---

[24]I want to thank professor Lars Hertzberg and his seminar for valuable criticism of
earlier drafts of this chapter.

4 Time and values

Juha Räikkä [1]

According to common wisdom, our values have changed. Nevertheless, there is little agreement as to whether this change has been positive. This chapter reviews some positions relevant to the question of whether our values have improved or deteriorated. Although the discussion does not concentrate on any particular theorist, it is obviously closely connected to John Rawls' views about ethical evaluation and Francis Fukuyama's views about history and progress.[2]

Contemporary western values

Many people currently claim that a remarkable change in values has occurred during the last ten to fifteen years.[3] Contemporary Western values, beliefs or emotions concerning the question of what is valuable are said to be very different from how they were, for example, in the 1970's. Three claims commonly accompany this position:

1. We are at present in the midst of a value crisis.

2. There are no longer any values in the West.

3. We are currently faced with too many different values.

---

[1] Warm thanks are due to John F. Corvino of the Department of Philosophy, University of Texas at Austin, for improving the English of this chapter.

[2] Rawls (1971), Rawls (1993), Fukuyama (1989), Fukuyama (1992).

[3] Newspapers and TV broadcasts are common sources for the claim that our values have changed dramatically, but the claim is present in more theoretical discussions as well. See e.g. O'Neill (1988).

All of these claims are somehow related to the view that *commercial values*, i.e. strongly individual values which have traditionally shaped life only in the marketplace, have penetrated other spheres. But what exactly is meant by these claims? They can obviously be interpreted in many different ways, and this fact may be one reason for their popularity. First of all, it is unclear what is meant by 'we'. Does the Western 'we' include everyone who lives in the West whatever 'the West' means or does it only include some Western people, say, politicians or youth? Secondly, it is unclear what 'having values' means. If one has a value, does one have to act in a certain way, or is it enough to *believe* or to *feel* a certain way? Finally, we do not know what 'values' are. If we grant that a value is a property of a thing, does everything that we suppose to be valuable actually have value or are so called 'higher' values, i.e. moral and aesthetic values, the only 'real' values?[4]

1. Let us first consider the claim that western culture is undergoing a value crisis. This view can be interpreted as a claim that we are not currently given alternatives to mainstream political views (values). In particular, current economic policy and its resulting unemployment are accepted uncritically as the only possibility. There is no discussion of underlying values, and thus political action consists of nothing but policy-making. We are in a crisis. On this interpretation, 'Western people' (i.e. 'we') does not refer to everyone in the West; rather, it refers to politicians and other politically active persons. Furthermore, 'having values' means acting in a certain way – it is not enough merely to believe or to feel something. Finally, on this interpretation, what is considered valuable are certain political viewpoints and their anticipated results. Interestingly, however, there are two further implications of the notion that we are in a value crisis. First, it implies that things are different now from the way they used to be. A change has occurred. Second, it implies that this change is for the worse. We are in a 'crisis' – hence, in trouble.

2. What about the second claim, that there are no longer any values in the West? One reasonable interpretation of this claim is that certain kinds of values are no longer popular in the West. Certain traditional values, like the values of solidarity and community, no longer have any significant effect on people. Instead, they have been replaced by commercial values, which now determine not only life in the marketplace but also life at home and at work.[5] On this interpretation of the second claim, 'Western people' are first of all young people who live in the West. Older people, i.e., the

---

[4]Obviously, the notion of value has many senses beyond just the moral and the aesthetic. See e.g. Frondizi (1971).

[5]Regarding the relation between politics and economical decisions and systems, see Acton (1971); or George (1982, 89-108).

prewar generation, may still respect some traditional values (e.g. the value of community) but not respect others. 'Having a value' here means believing in something, rather than acting in a certain way. The difference between generations is not so much in their habits as in their attitudes. And the concept of value, on this interpretation, refers to so-called 'higher' values. Certain moral values are no longer accepted, while others (e.g. the value of nourishment) are generally as accepted as before. Again there are two further points to be made: first, the situation is different from before, and second, the situation is worse than before – for surely it is better to have values than not to have them.

3. The third claim is that we are currently faced with too many different values. How is it possible that at the same time there are no values (second claim) and too many values? Obviously, the third claim means something like the following: it is difficult to judge what is valuable, given the plurality of alternatives. In simple terms, it is as if one could walk into a shop and buy one's own religion, one's own ethical system, and one's own *Weltanshauung*; practically anything can be bought. Social control over habits and lifestyles is a thing of the past: we are free – indeed, too free for comfort. This interpretation sees 'Western people' as all those who live in the West – at least, almost every Western person is Western on this view. 'Having a value' on this interpretation means having a tendency to choose certain things over others. Furthermore, there is no restriction on what can be chosen: one might pursue 'higher values,' but one might also value material goods, travel, a certain football team, and so on. Not surprisingly, the third claim also implies that this plurality of values has not always existed, the situation is brand new. Furthermore, like the first and second, the third claim implies that the situation is bad. There are not merely many values; there are too many values. We can draw the following five conclusions concerning contemporary Western ideas about values:

1. Alternative political (value) positions are not considered.

2. Traditional 'higher' values have largely lost their force.

3. Value judgements are complicated because of the plurality of values.

4. The situation is different from what it used to be.

5. The situation is worse than it used to be.

Are these claims justified? Answering this question would require many further specifications. However, it seems that all of them are intuitively plausible, while at the same time, all of them can be criticized. To take just one example: while it is certainly true that grandparents do not value exactly the same things as their grandchildren, it is hardly the case that grandchildren do not respect *any* of their grandparents' values *at all*. Note that the fifth claim is markedly different from the first four. The first four claims comprise an empirical thesis marked by the idea that commercial values, which were once present only in the marketplace, have penetrated political, social, and personal spheres as well. The fifth claim, on the other hand, is a value judgement. It states that the penetration of commercial values is a bad thing.[6]

Time, values and evaluation

How might we defend the view that our values today are worse than they used to be? How might we prove that the penetration of commercial values into other spheres is itself of negative value? How might we justify the assertion that the current values are bad? There are four possible grounds for such a judgement:

1. Values in the past.

2. Values in the future.

3. Eternal, ahistorical values.

4. The current values themselves

   It is clear that we need some ground for value judgements. If this ground is historical, then it is in the past, present or future. The alternative is that the ground is in some way ahistorical.[7]
   1. Consider the first alternative. It may seem reasonable to refer to the values of the past in criticizing current values. Obviously, traditional community-centered values conflict somewhat with more business-oriented, egoistic values. If we trust in old values, it appears to follow both that something is wrong today and that nothing was wrong yesterday. Moreover, there are numerous examples of this practice of referring to the past. People often assert that our grandparents would be ashamed of our ways, and that

---

[6]The claim that the penetration of commercial values is a bad thing is defended especially keenly by Georg Henrik von Wright in his recent public talks.

[7]In a sense, the fifth alternative is that moral 'time-relativism' is true, i.e. that there is no way to evaluate values of times other than our own. (It would be interesting to explore what meaning could be given to 'our own' given 'time-relativism.') For a discussion of different versions of moral relativism, see Wong (1984).

our current needs are illusory, since people in the past did not share them. Both lines of argument refer to the past: people then knew better.

But can we justify the practice of grounding criticism of current values in the values of the past? Clearly not. First, if we grant that our contemporaries can be mistaken about what is really valuable – a point presupposed by the view that our values have deteriorated – then we must also allow that our parents and grandparents may have been mistaken, since there is no difference between them and us with regard to the ability to know what is truly valuable. Second, there is no monolithic entity that can justifiably be labeled as 'the values of the past' – people have always disagreed about what is valuable. For example, consider the assertion that people once valued solidarity. An equally reasonable assertion is that people once disvalued solidarity. Thus past values may not only provide criticism for current values, but also praise.

2. But what about the second alternative? Is it perhaps more reasonable to refer to values in the future in order to criticize values in the present? Like past values, future values will no doubt conflict with current ones. Surely our values will not remain the same forever; they will change to some degree. Therefore, if we know that something will be valued in the future, why not value it right now? Interestingly, this line of argument is fairly common. For example, some geneticists argue that it is pointless to set limits on their research, since future generations will not even imagine that such research could be dangerous. Indeed, one might claim that current arguments for limiting genetic research are as absurd as past arguments against train travel, which rested on the idea that trains are too fast to be safe. Just as we now know that trains are useful, we will someday realize that genetic research is useful – hence there is no good reason to limit it today.

Is this sort of reasoning credible? Hardly. First of all, we do not know what values will be accepted in the future. An argument that depends upon such knowledge is at best uncertain, for although our predictions may be correct, they may also be incorrect. Secondly, even if we knew for certain what values will be accepted in the future, the people of the future could be mistaken. Since we are (and always have been) fallible with regard to values, future generations will likely be so as well. There is no reason to expect that they will discover how to justify values any better than we do. Thus it might be unwise to trust the views of future people, even if such views were currently available. We therefore must reject this alternative.

3. Reference to ahistorical or transhistorical values is another possible strategy for criticizing current values. 'Ahistorical' can be understood in two ways: either as 'ever-present', that is, not related to any *specific* period of time, or as 'beyond time,' that is, not related to time at all; neither present,

past, nor future. Ahistorical values may well differ from current ones, and the more they differ, the better grounds they provide for criticism. Moreover, people frequently appeal to ahistorical values – or more precisely, to values which they believe to be ahistorical. For example, some 'pro-lifers' argue that abortion is morally wrong because (they believe that) God condemns it. Similarly, human rights activists argue that certain political systems are immoral because (according to them) these systems violate absolute human rights – moral rights that are ever-present in humans.

Does this strategy work? It seems more credible than the previous two, insofar as it allows that people can always be mistaken about what is valuable.[8] Such fallibility is an important intuition concerning values – mistakes are possible for anyone, past, present or future. But reference to ahistorical values also has its problems, the primary one being that we do not know which ahistorical values are correct. Although some people believe in Judeo-Christian values, others find them, if not ridiculous, at least obviously wrong. If there were some method for discerning correct values, such disagreement would not present a problem. But no such method is available, and this strategy therefore fails.

4. The fourth and last alternative for criticizing current values is to ground the criticism in the current values themselves. At first glance this strategy appears impossible. Surely, judging current values by their own standards is tantamount to saying they are perfectly acceptable, is it not? Not exactly. It is possible to criticize *some* current values on the grounds of *some other* current values. This possibility exists because contemporary values hardly comprise a coherent set.

People discussing values, especially political and moral values, typically refer to those that are accepted *at present*. Consider, for example, 19th century criticisms of the American institution of slavery. At the time, it was a generally accepted belief that persons are, metaphysically speaking, free, i.e. they have the *right* to be free. Opponents of slavery appealed to this belief, arguing that slavery – which entails denial of various freedoms – cannot be justified in light of it. It cannot be the case both that people are free and that slavery is justifiable. So criticism of one 19th century value – that of slavery – was justified by appealing to another 19th century value – that of freedom.

Note as well that many arguments which are purportedly based on past, future, or ahistorical values are actually based on current values. We tend to invoke former and future values only if we value them on our current

---

[8]This is perhaps the main reason why finding ahistorical values has been judged so important. See Dworkin (1983, 4-6); or Brandt (1990, 259-278).

scale. Indeed, referring to the past as 'the *good* old days' or to the future as '*progress*' necessarily involves a *current* value judgement about either. And so-called 'ahistorical' values are frequently if not always currently popular as well.

The best approach for criticizing current values seems to be to employ other current values as the basis of the critique.[9] This alternative avoids the problems faced by the others, and in fact is the strategy most commonly used. There is an interesting conclusion to be drawn from this argument, namely, that it is impossible for *all* current values to be bad. At least, many people do trust many current values. (Of course, it is possible for two conflicting values to be both wrong.) If current values are bad – as they may well be – they are only partly so. Hence the view that current values are worse than those of the past is at best only partly correct – there is no cause for panic. The penetration of commercial values is not as serious a problem as is supposed.

Have our values progressed?

If we grant that not all of our values are bad, can we go further and claim that our values have progressed? Many people today believe the opposite – that our values have not progressed, but rather, deteriorated. Others, however, have suggested that values progress in time.[10] There are several variants[11] to this view, most of which share the following premises:

1. Our values have converged.

2. Convergence of values indicates progress

If both of these claims are justified, then the view that contemporary Western values are bad, even if only partially, is wrong. Rather, Western values have progressed, and the penetration of commercial values has been positive. Let us therefore explore whether these claims are in fact justified.

1. Consider the convergence thesis first. This thesis is an empirical claim that Western values have converged at both the social and personal level. According to this view, western societies have largely accepted liberal governing principles. Pluralism is widely valued, and even traditional socialists admit problems with the claim that a government can know better than people themselves what comprises a good life or what is truly valuable. In addition,

---

[9]Of course, the view that criticism of current values can be based on current values themselves is anything but uncontroversial. See e.g. Brandt (1979, 20-22).

[10]See for instance Daniels (1979, 256-282).

[11]For an alternative to Daniels, see Francis Fukuyama, op.cit. (note 2).

according to the convergence thesis, personal values are at the background of the convergence of societal values. Even if all Western societies still contain fascists, communists, Christians and liberals, persons from these various traditions seem to accept that even if the other traditions are obviously wrong, it is neither reasonable nor morally justifiable to try to compel their members to change.

The convergence thesis is easily defended. That Western values have converged at both the social and personal levels is hardly so complex that we cannot see fairly straightforward empirical evidence on its behalf. For instance, the legal systems of various societies are obviously more similar than they once were. Furthermore, the political strategies of the radical left and right are becoming largely similar to those of mainstream political movements.

The only possible objections to the convergence thesis are first, that convergence has happened on too short a time scale to be probative, and second, that the convergence has been merely formal and not substantial in character. Perhaps we should wait, say, one hundred years, and then judge whether our values have converged. Or perhaps the apparent convergence of values is only formal in character, that is, values are still understood quite differently even if a common discourse is employed when discussing them. Perhaps North Americans and Poles, for instance, have incompatible ideas about democracy, even if their laws currently resemble each other. Despite these objections (which would deserve further attention), however, the convergence thesis remains plausible, if not unproblematic. Therefore, if the second premise is correct – if convergence indicates progress – then our values may have progressed, and not merely changed.

2. Does convergence indicate progress? Those who say that it does can point to the fact that generally, when people largely agree on something, they consider that something to be justified. In empirical or scientific matters this method of justification works - so why not in matters of value as well? To a certain extent agreement seems to have justificatory power in itself. If everyone agrees on a particular viewpoint, then that viewpoint has intersubjective support, and many think that intersubjectivity is the only reasonable meaning of objectivity. So if people now agree on pluralistic, liberal values, this agreement may be a sign that such values are justified.

One can of course attempt to counteract the thesis that convergence indicates progress by appealing to familiar counterarguments against the consensus theory of truth and justification. Naturally, agreement and justification are very different things. Sometimes people are perfectly happy with beliefs that are nevertheless wrong, and people agree about all kinds of things.[12] Hence it would be foolish to decide by majority vote which beliefs are epistemically correct. Although this argument reveals problems with the convergence thesis, it is not devastating. Even if agreement and justification are different, 'shared opinion' in fact has a positive correlation with 'justified opinion.' Thus it is still possible for convergence of values to provide evidence that current values are correct.

There is another problem, however, with the argument that our values are improving because convergence implies progress. This argument presupposes not only that convergence occurred in the past, but also that it will continue to occur in the future. If indeed our values are progressing because they are converging – and not merely because they have converged during a specific period – then our future values will also converge. But is this empirical speculation well taken? What evidence do we have for or against such a view? Almost none. Thus the claim that values are progressing can be justified at best in a modified form, according to which our values *have* progressed. And if in the future our values fail to converge, perhaps we will then say that they never converged at all – the convergence was only seeming.

Let us draw some conclusions, emphasizing two points. First, the common view that laments the fact that commercial values have increasingly gained ground in the West rests on an exaggeration. Even if we admit that alternative political policies are not discussed, that political decisions are influenced by economic factors, that traditional moral values have lost their force because commercial values have infiltrated the home, and that value judgements are more complex now than they once were, we need not conclude that current values are altogether bad. Rather, we must judge them mainly by current standards – the current values themselves.

Secondly, the view that Western values are progressing because they have converged is not credible. Even if we accept that all Western societies embrace both value pluralism and the penetration of commercial values, we can still deny that our values are progressing, for convergence does not necessarily imply progress. In the future our values may diverge as well as converge – we do not know which.

---

[12]Cf. Raz (1982, 307-330).

5   Having an economy

Elizabeth Wolgast

What does it mean to have an economy? Must this be an aspect of a community, or do only certain societies have an economy? How do we know whether a community has one or not, must it be distinct from other aspects of life – religion and politics for instance? These are my questions.

i.

Imagine a tribe like this one. Its members get their food by hunting and gathering; they make clothes of hides and a coarse fabric they weave, and pottery from local clay; they build houses from branches, and carry water from nearby streams. Whatever the tribe cannot find or hunt or make, it gets along without. Nothing is intentionally produced in advance and little is stored; supplies are found or made when they are needed.

The members' activities are divided like this. The young and mature men hunt, gather wood, and maintain the boats and tools needed for these, while young and mature women cook, weave, and make pottery. Children led by some mature member pick and sort food; elderly men tan hides and assist in judicial and some other matters; elderly women watch the very young children. When a group is finished its designated activity, it joins other groups with theirs. When they judge their productive activities complete they join in rituals to propitiate the gods, or tell stories, most connected with their rituals and beliefs; and they play games. One might say that traditions govern a great deal of their lives, and dictate the priorities in most situations. The people look on these ways as necessary to a prosperous life.

Such a general schematic picture is fairly familiar to anthropologists who study small tribal communities, sometimes called 'primitive communities'.

Using English I might describe their lives in terms of work, play, worship, etc., but there is no way to demarcate these within their lives, for instance, they don't treat dancing much differently from other activities. All are serious, you might say – all have a place and importance in their lives and are seamlessly joined, a fact we find reflected in their language.

The tribe has a council of priests which decides (among other things) what the community's activities will be and how they should be divided, which group should do what and when. It also settles disputes whenever they arise. These are rare, however, for normally the members live peacefully and view their community as happy and fortunate, one favored by the gods. They have no trade with other communities but at certain seasons they join for celebrations with their neighbors.

This description is not meant to be complete, for instance I've said nothing much about the tribe's family life, and nothing about its standard of living – if that term applies. But the description serves to frame the question, does the tribe have an economy and how do we determine this?

Consider the two answers, yes and no (perhaps there are others). No: the tribe has no economy for a variety of reasons, each connected with what might be called a criterion for having one.

First, the "management of resources" is one standard definition of an economy. Yet it is clearly difficult to identify a set of "resources" which are "managed" here. Second, money is often associated with economics, but the tribe has no medium of exchange, tokens or beads or other things that might be used the way money is. One reason is that there is *no exchange* of goods, not even barter. People offer presents on ceremonial occasions, of course, most notably when a young couple marries, and the choice of gifts may have some significance. But there is no exchanging which would allow one to speak of fair exchange, and no agreement about the values of things.

Exchange is absent partly because of the view the tribe has of their lives and relation to the deities. Living as I described, they find no place for acquiring material things except what they acquire as a community. It should be noted here, however, that if some kind of exchange – for instance a system of barter – is required to have an economy, other communities besides my tribe may have none: a self-sufficient monastery might not. I will return to this later.

Third, the specialization of work which often goes with a system of exchange, is also missing. What specialization exists does so only in the sense that a person's work follows the lines of sex and age that determine all activities. If one person is very skillful at a task, others admire and appreciate that talent, but there is no reward for superior skills, and no choosing or preferring such a person when a given job is needed. An emphasis like that would discriminate against the less talented, they think.

Fourth, it follows that nothing corresponds to our idea of *demand* for goods or services. Expressions of desire to have something are very rare, and reproached as immature whining. The members believe it is impious to want more than is provided and available. Notice that a monastic society may be like this too.

Finally, as I explained, there is no way to separate anything we might call 'economic' activity from the rest of this tribe's life. Work, like rituals, is both necessary and sacred, the one no more than the other. Indeed, *all* their activities are continuous with their religion, which is in turn connected with their expectation of prospering in the future and their sense of well being. One might even say that they lack a concept of work, since everything they do is connected with position and the tribal rules on the one hand, and with religion and their relation to the world on the other. Without a line separating leisure and work, both concepts – work and leisure – might be considered inapplicable. When we describe their way of life we use these words, but as our account increases in understanding, we emphasize qualifications in using them. In the same way religion is not a distinguishable aspect of their lives either, and our remarks about it must also be qualified.

Notice that many of these features might characterize certain monastic communities as well, but there is an important difference: the monastic order would presumably understand and use a language in which there were the expressions "our economy," "our religion". Thus, if the leader or patriarch were asked about the monastery's economy, e.g. 'what kind is it?', he would presumably understand what was asked for. He might answer that their economy consists in growing their own food and bartering the surplus for other things they need, etc., and so acknowledge an economic aspect of their lives. He implies that the monastery has an economy.

But he might instead reject the question saying that they don't think in such terms, that they view everything they have as given by God and everything they do, down to the humblest details, as part of lives in the service of God. For instance, the yield of their garden is not seen as the result of effort but a gift from heaven, their participation in its growth a bond with God, and so on. In such ways their situation resembles that of my tribe. The difference is that the tribe cannot understand the question while the monastic members can.

ii.

That is how the negative answer goes; now look at the affirmative one. Yes, one might argue, they have an economy because any community must have an economy in some form. It must because an economy is simply the way a society satisfies its material needs, and some of these are vital. To deny that my tribe has an economy is therefore to deny that it satisfies essential needs, which is absurd. One should say that this community's economy is founded on group accomplishment of tasks for the benefit of all, it is a form of socialism under the direction of a council. The lack of money or other medium of exchange is not crucial; what is important is the activities they engage in to satisfy their needs: these are what we call economic. One could say something similar for the monastic community. Let us spell out the argument further.

Material needs of humans are not defined arbitrarily. Having certain kinds of foods is not optional for a viable community, but vitally important. It follows, or seems to, that there must also be such a thing as demand even in that context, and that people's lives and the form of the community will reflect these needs somehow. In my tribe where activities are specified by the council, the problem seems to lie in the description as I gave it – perhaps it lacks details of how the council considers the people's material needs and takes account of them. We can be sure they affect its thinking somehow.

The affirmative answer reflects the belief that an economy will be a feature of any human society, any society of creatures really, since all will have needs which have to be met and ways of meeting them. There is no further argument about my society, however infused its ideas of material needs are with religious meaning. It can no more avoid having one than it can avoid the need for food, or for clothes in a cold climate. This explains why dictionaries speak of the management of resources: it is assumed that, humans being as they are, there must be resources of certain kinds for them to survive and these must be managed somehow.

I suggest against this argument that it's unclear what force this 'must' has. What constitutes a human 'need', what counts as 'resources', as 'production', 'work'? And what determines the answers? Think how one might draw a line between the tribe's economy and other aspects of its life. Where would we put it? Not between their economy and their religion, for religion informs all their ideas about life including their attitude toward what we call their needs. True, they eat food that we call 'needed', but their thinking does not use this category. You might say that their religion incorporates their entire ethos in the Greek sense, for it is of a piece with everything else in their lives. Which means that we cannot use our own conceptions of these straightforwardly, and no matter how translations are made they will not constitute a description that harmonizes with the way the tribe sees and describe itself. Nor will it be how a sympathetic observer would describe them. The terms don't translate without distortion from a foreign framework.

Compare the question about the tribe's economy to the corresponding question: Does the tribe have a political system? They have a council that makes decisions regarding the community, and this gives a reason for saying yes. However here too interconnections obtrude, for there is continuity between the governing and religious functions of the council, and calling some of them political, others religious, still others judicial would ignore the way that the religious authority creates and colors authority of other kinds, and the institutions themselves. A council member does not speak in a purely secular capacity, that idea makes no sense. We face again the problem regarding its economy: On the one hand we want to say that having a political system is a universal and distinct feature of a community, yet it isn't clear how this necessity can be made palpable for the tribe.

Since religion is no more a distinct aspect of the tribe's life than an economy is, we should perhaps not say that it has a religion either. This strikes one as plausible once one understands the interconnections. A similar indissoluble connection may hold in a monastic order: does it not have a religion then? Saying that it does is too lean to express the importance of religion to everything about their lives. It might be better to say that their religion is coextensive with their lives; but then it is being distinguished from nothing. There is nothing secular, non-religious in their lives, and thus nothing distinctively religious either. That is like my tribe.

If we were anthropologists studying and comparing different cultures, we might use the term "economy" in our description of both the tribe and the monastery, might say that the latter's economy is partly agricultural, partly dependent on gifts from surrounding communities, partly on support from the larger church, etc. And we might say of the tribe's economy that it consists of hunting and gathering and simple manufacture. But to members of both, these descriptions would seem wrongly put, and they might say we had not understood their lives at all.

Let us go back to the beginning. If as it seems, both the answers yes and no to whether the tribe has an economy seem coherent, perhaps we should infer that it's not clear what 'economy' means outside of certain kinds of societies, certain ways of living and thinking. We could say that it may lack meaning for a non-modern, non-industrialized society, and thus the range of its unambiguous application is restricted. But this response seems to say that having an economy is already the sign of a certain kind of ethos and not separable from it. While we are accustomed to separate and distinguish different aspects of society and think of this procedure as natural and unequivocal, the fact is that this is a prejudice.

iii.

Distinguishing an economy from other aspects of social life belongs to a certain way of looking at society, belongs to a certain ethos: that is the point I am working toward. Take the idea that supply and demand are universally central driving forces. This assumption is informed by a conception of human desires, particularly for material things, and the respect they are accorded. If supply and demand have any power to explain how a society works, those presenting their wishes give importance to their fulfillment, while those who possess what is desired must treat those wishes with respect. The ideas and the respect are part of their ethos.

Further, the way desires or demands are treated will be seen in other facets of the community's life – in the connections between people and between them and the community, both of which will affect politics and be harmonized with religion, and so on. All these will constitute parts of the ethos: supply and demand belong to how these people view their lives and their relations to others, how they conceive their happiness, express their priorities, and play their lives out.

Imagine the objection that, whatever their language and way of thinking, an economy of some kind is necessary. The ethos of the tribe must give respect to supply and demand relations between people, it must make room for these. Yet in my tribe there was neither a supply-demand mechanism nor room for one, in that context the idea didn't make sense. And thus we found that talking about their economy was something like talking about property ownership in a community where all land is in common. We can do it only with great artificiality. The process would compare with the tribe's insistence that even in our society, religious ideas penetrate all other areas; that there are no boundaries between politics, religion, economics, however much we deny it.

One needs to be careful about using 'descriptive' language that carries implications into contexts where they don't belong. And what emerges from this is the idea that there may be no value-neutral language which we can use about other societies, and if we think that there must be one, that is also part of an ethos, namely our own.

Look again at the insistence that my tribe must have an economy at least in the minimal sense of satisfying generic physical needs. One can imagine that the tribe's ethos might even prohibit consumption of foods we deem necessary to existence, as it might prohibit sexual intercourse or procreation; the group's survival would then be hostage to these standards, but that is a real possibility. Neither biology nor philosophy can tell us what people must think, what they must make of their condition. The necessity of having an economy lies in our ethos, and we incorporate it into the picture we make of the tribe; but this move tends to make the discussion whether they have an economy vacuous.

I proposed that my tribe members cannot imagine themselves having requirements, that they frown on demands or requests made of the gods, for instance, and cannot imagine divinities who respond by supplying what people ask for. In the same way the attitudes and institutions that would correlate with our ideas of human necessities are missing: there is no way to explain such "necessities" to them. We face the conclusion that understanding the tribe's life is not furthered by thinking or speaking of its economy. There is a corollary: If the tribe did have something identifiable as an economy, its ethos would be different from what it is.

iv.

My aim in imagining the tribe was to ask if we can always make coherent the possession of an economy, and my conclusion is that it becomes increasingly incoherent as the aspects we distinguish increasingly merge or become assimilated to one cardinal set of ideas and values. Unless one insists that it remains a necessary or tautologous feature, one tends to say that the meaning of "economy" loses its customary grip. Now I ask whether this procedure is legitimate.

My method takes as touchstone Wittgenstein's saying that understanding a language means understanding a way of life, by which I take him to mean that language and practices, words and the ways people live are synergistic, they are co-dependent and inseparable. Thus their language is tightly interwoven with contexts and activities, with the way they live in every sense. This means that abstract questions and pronouncements which are detached from such settings become inherently suspect.

Following this suggestion, I am asking whether having an economy would make sense in a way of living very different from those in which the term now has regular and indispensable employment. Does it make sense applied to a society without a vital focus on selling and buying, getting, spending and consuming we are accustomed to. I am drawn toward the negative answer.

However there remains another source of insisting that it must make sense; it is a view of human nature that is held by many modern economists.

That view takes human needs and desires and their satisfaction as important aspects of any human life, and as representing fundamental, timeless, universal human values. Thus it is maintained that these needs and values must frame an economy however they are expressed in particular institutions and customs. The setting and institutions vary from place to place and time to time, but the incorporation of them somehow in life is unavoidable. From this standpoint, we see society as a collection of need-seeking individuals joined together only by self-interest. For such beings their economy is a crucial way of relating to each other.

Such is the vision of Hobbes and Locke, and it pervades much of the thinking of our time. Let us see how its assumptions are spelled out. Consider the idea that life is centered around satisfying needs and desires, and the idea that these form the basis for human interactions. In this picture, a person is happy to the degree that her desires are satisfied, unhappy to the degree they are not. This may really describe people with a certain ethos: they may actually be, and consider others, happy depending on whether their personal desires are satisfied. But this vision is incomprehensible to my tribe, and if they could understand it they would deny it's truth. As certain as economists are that it is right, they are confident it is misguided. True happiness (they say) means living in the benevolent aspect of the gods, and cannot imagine that satisfying desires, idiosyncratic or even harmful, has any connection with happiness. Even hunger and deprivation may have a positive meaning.

The economist Milton Friedman claims to see any voluntary action as the expression of some desire: if a person did not want to do a thing, he argues, she would not do it, having no motive to. Thus, Friedman would see my tribe's participation in rituals as motivated by desire just as much as other actions, here the desire to show respect for the gods. The connection between acting voluntarily and desiring is tautological, he would say. This lays the groundwork for concepts that go hand in hand with the desire satisfaction-motive – exchange, supply, demand, value, production. It also lays the ground for competition as a natural way for people to associate.

I am arguing that our conception of economics is parochial. The question, Where is the dividing line between a society's economy and its religion or politics? leads me to respond that it is impossible to say out of context. It is part of the ethos of some people to speak this way and treat economic concepts as palpable. Even the idea that there is a line distinguishing economic from non-economic matters is a myth, part of the ethos.

The right conclusion to draw is that any answer to the question must be understood in the context of one's own view of what a society is and what sort of beings humans are. This means that seeing economics as a crucial aspect of society is not particularly scientific, not because (as is sometimes protested) there can be no experiments or laws or sound predictions, but because distinguishing an economy this way is part of a view of human life that others need not share. And the categories of that view will be linked indissolubly with a distinct way of life.

My principal conclusion is that some terms are so closely reflective of an ethos that they cannot apply to communities that are radically different. The idea that they can be used neutrally or "objectively" is an illusion embedded in talk about the "science" of economics. But as we describe societies very unlike ours, our language should be under scrupulous surveillance, as should the tendency to treat a social vision as scientific.

At this point one might be inclined to propose a very odd query, namely, whether our ways of thinking about society, and distinguishing separate areas of social life – religion, politics, economics – is more enlightened than a way like my tribe's which doesn't separate them. Offhand it is unclear that such a question as it stands makes any sense. At the very least it is baffling: from what standpoint could we raise and debate it, from what position can we criticize our own ethos? Criticism, if we are to engage in it, must come from inside our view of society and ourselves, that is the only view we have. At the same time it must be acknowledged that if we feel any objection to how our view works, it is also from within our view that we feel it.

What looks like a paradox here might be resolved by showing that our ethos contains different strands or motifs, and that some of them may be discordant with the division of life into separate aspects. Once this is accepted, it also appears possible that we prefer some ways of seeing things – and its implications – to other ways. In that case criticizing our own vision becomes conceivable: it becomes imaginable that we should live and think and talk in a way we don't. It becomes imaginable that we might live and speak in a way that makes no place for an economy with its penetrating implications and assumptions. This intriguing possibility, however, I offer as nothing more than a speculative afterthought.

6 'What a waste!'

Lars Hertzberg

1.   A few years ago I made a visit to San Xavier del Bac, a striking Spanish colonial church shining white in the brown Arizona desert near Tucson. The congregation consists mainly of Pima Indians apparently living in destitute conditions in a nearby village. In a room adjacent to the main church hall there was a plain cylindrical aluminium container with a tap. Attached to the container was the note: 'Don't waste holy water!'

The note made me curious. Why would such a warning be needed? Why did one have to fear the waste? Is not holy water just ordinary tap water that has been consecrated? After all there should be plenty of raw material. I do not know what the Catholic ceremonial for consecrating water is, but I would imagine that if a shortage were to arise, one could just consecrate some more. And I knew that the water table in the desert was sinking, but what difference could a few ounces of holy water make, compared, for instance, to the huge consumption of water taking place in the nearby city? To be sure, the congregation was poor, but it could not be that poor.

Only later did I realize how fatuous my first reaction had been. The terms in which I had thought about the admonition were the expression of an impoverished sense of economy and waste. The reason people were told to be economical with the water, of course, need have had nothing to do with economics, that is, it need not have been based on a calculation. On the contrary, it could be regarded as an expression of *what it meant* to regard the water as holy, a reminder that there were certain ways of using it (say, for washing up, watering plants or filling a squirt gun) that would have been incompatible with the reverence due to the water. In fact, it could be said that the holiness of holy water consists precisely in such differences in the attitude with which holy and ordinary water is used, and the way these differences connect with the contrast between the concerns of church ritual

103

and everyday life. If someone were unable to see the need to use the water sparingly in anything but economic terms, this would simply mean that its holiness had no significance for him.

In speaking of my 'impoverished sense of economy and waste' just now, I was suggesting that this is a way of thinking to which members of contemporary Western civilization are particularly prone. We live in a culture in which economic forms of thought hold a dominant position in public discourse (along, for instance, with scientific and administrative forms of thought). Quite naturally, these forms of thought will also tend to colour the ways in which individuals think about their own lives. While human motives and activities can be regarded from a variety of perspectives, we are inclined to give a high priority to considerations of cost, return on investment, long-term profits, etc. (This is not to say that contemporary Westerners are particularly greedy, as compared to people at other times or in other cultures; I have grave doubts about the meaningfulness of any such comparison: what it means is simply that we have a tendency to view all kinds of problems from this particular angle).[1]

The question why this has come to be so is large and complicated. It is probably to be seen as the result of a process of give-and-take, in which certain prominent attitudes (say, a traditional European emphasis on virtues like thrift and industry) have interacted with factors such as population growth, geography, technological innovation and the opportunity for trade, to bring about a form of social and economic organization (industrialization, the monetary economy) in which attention to economic considerations is a condition for civic success.

Because of this, the economic perspective on life is not one that we are free either to retain or to discard like a pair of glasses. It would be an illusion to suppose that we could simply cease to be economics-minded without a radical concurrent change in our whole way of life. This does not mean, however, that we may not strive to become aware of the limitations of this perspective, of the ways in which it may distort matters or the things it may tend to hide from our sight. For even if we have a tendency to see things from an economic point of view, we are not incapable of regarding things in other ways as well. In this essay, I wish to use the concept of waste as a way of exploring some of the ways in which the economic perspective tends to

---

[1] The interdependence between culture and human motives is a complex one. Of course, in a culture in which everything is discussed in economic terms, the line between greed and more respectable motives will be harder to make out, may even, in some cases, dissolve altogether. But on the other hand, in such a culture non-economic motives will tend to be dressed up in economic garb, and accordingly the mercenary side of human motivation may come to seem larger than it is.

distort our view of human action.

2.   In fact most of us, I believe, have reactions to waste that are not economically circumscribed. Thus, people are often reluctant to throw away left-over
food or used clothing. In the apple season, people with apple trees will often
get more apples than they can eat or store. They may then give them to
friends or neighbours, even put them on carts by the roadside for passers-by
to help themselves, rather than throw them away. There is clearly a feeling
that in this way the apples will not be wasted. Here considerations of waste
play a role that is not connected to economic calculation; for the apples that
are given away are placed outside the economy of the giver's needs no less
than if they had been thrown away.

Perhaps it will be claimed that economic calculation could still play a
part here, since the person who gives the apples away probably expects some
more or less indirect, maybe intangible return. Probably this description
will fit some instances, but to argue that all cases *must* be of this kind is
simply to express an *a priori* determination to regard all human behaviour
as expressive of economic calculations.[2] I should like to suggest that such a
determination is just another symptom of the impoverished sense of economy
and waste of which I spoke before.

In what follows, I want to take a look at some of the ways the word 'waste'
is used in everyday argument, in appraising and deliberating on human action. What will be seen is that in many of the contexts in which the word is
used, its significance cannot be spelled out in economic terms.

3.   Suppose a wife accuses her husband of having wasteful habits, say, of
driving a car which guzzles too much petrol, or spending too much time and
money at the pub, betting on horses, or the like. He might perhaps defend his
habits by denying that they are as expensive as she thinks, or by pointing to
possible benefits from them (driving an expensive car is good for his image,
speaking to business acquaintances at the pub is essential for his work, etc).

The discussion that might take place in such a case is similar to one that
might be carried on concerning the practices of a business company. The
company's accountants might point out that some of its practices are wasteful: it would, for instance, be able to cut down on transport costs by hiring

---

[2]The 'intangible returns' envisaged by economic theorists as a way of upholding the
universality of the economic motive are somewhat reminiscent of the epicycles introduced
by the Hellenistic astronomer Ptolemy in order to render the apparent motion of the
planets compatible with the *a priori* requirement that celestial movements had to be
circular.

transport services from a carrier rather than investing money in its own lorries and drivers (or the other way round). Waste, here, is a relative notion: what makes one practice wasteful is simply the fact that an alternative practice can be clearly shown to be less costly. On the other hand, such criticism might conceivably be countered by pointing out that there are indirect gains from the current practice (say, employing its own drivers makes the company less vulnerable to fluctuations in the transport market, marketing benefits can be attained by having lorries display the company brand name, etc.).

4. Another line of defence would be for the husband to argue that he can *afford* his expensive habits: his incomes are good enough so that he can go on indulging them without the family being forced to cut down on anything essential. Here too, in a different sense, the question of waste becomes relative: what is considered wasteful becomes a matter of what one can or cannot afford, of what is 'economically possible'. Let us consider more closely what is involved in this notion of economic possibility.[3]

The notion of not being able to afford something will involve a continuum of cases. If I tell you I cannot afford to buy a certain house, I may mean that, however much I might want to buy it or however important I consider the purchase, the money or credits available to me are simply not sufficient to enable me to come up with the purchase-sum. There is nothing I can do, within the bounds of the law, that would make me the proprietor of the house. We might call this a limiting case of what it means not to be able to afford something. But I may also mean that (although I could come up with the money) the economic consequences of buying it would be unacceptable.

---

[3]We should note that this line of defence would hardly be available to a business corporation. Defending a cost-inefficient practice on the grounds that the company can afford it would probably be considered the height of irresponsibility (which does not mean that such practices will not in fact exist). This is not so simply because a business corporation is supposed to be maximizing its profits; the same is true of public institutions funded with taxpayers' money such as schools or hospitals, or non-profit organizations such as the International Red Cross which are dependent on private and public contributions. Organizations like these, in our culture, are subject to an ethic in which they are seen as mere instruments shaped and used for some purpose or range of purposes; unlike the individuals working in them, they do not have needs of their own: invoking the needs of an organization is only legitimate if it can be justified by reference to its purposes. This means, too, that the question of what such an organization can afford cannot arise in the same way as in the case of private persons. Of course one may ask whether or not a company can afford to make such and such an investment, but only in the sense: is it able to come up with the money required? The question could not even be raised unless the investment were thought to be sound. (It may be said, on occasion, that a company can afford the losses it has had to endure. This would mean simply that it will not be brought to bankruptcy by them, not that the losses could have been accepted in advance.)

In an extreme case, it might mean that I would have no money left over for living expenses, or that I could then no longer fulfill my commitments to my family, or maintain a standard of living I consider essential, or that buying it would force me to give up certain things that I am not prepared to give up, etc.

In other words, at one end of the spectrum, there is, it appears, an economic impossibility that can be unambiguously seen to hold, given the legal and economic institutions of our society, whereas, as we move further away from this end, the judgement of what is possible is seen to be increasingly dependent on the way a person regards her life, on her priorities, on what she finds tolerable or intolerable, etc.[4] We define who we are, in part, in terms of what we consider possible or impossible for us. And our judgements of economic necessity or impossibility are embedded in this.

'So you are saying that a judgement of economic possibility is objective at one extreme, becoming increasingly subjective as we move towards the other extreme?' This way of putting the matter is all right, provided we do not misconstrue the contrast between 'the objective' and 'the subjective'. We are perhaps tempted to think of it as a contrast between what is independent of a person's attitude and what is determined by it. I would argue that this is misleading to the extent that the contrast (as it is drawn in this context) is not itself independent of human attitudes. An example should make this clearer: suppose someone's claim to be unable to come up with the money to buy a house encounters the rejoinder that of course he can do it: all he has to do is rob a bank, forge a signature on a cheque, or sell his daughters into prostitution. Our likely reaction to this rejoinder is to regard it as a rather feeble joke (it might even be understood as a hyperbolic way of underscoring the impossibility of collecting the money). For many of us, the possibilities mentioned here are not 'real' possibilities. They are things we do not think about. Among us, invoking them has no intelligible place in serious argument.[5]

Still there are of course communities (subcultures in our society or alien cultures) in which such methods will be seriously considered. (No claims of superiority are being made here. Among the things we would not seriously consider there may be some that we find admirable.) What does the difference between such communities and our own consist in? There may be no external difference between them, such as the danger of being caught robbing

---

[4]There is a similar continuum of cases where we speak about being forced (not) to do something, or about (not) having the time or the strength to do something.

[5]It is important to be clear that the question of what we are able to take seriously is not to be understood as psychological: it concerns the conditions for making oneself understood by others.

a bank. Nor does a person's readiness to give his daughters over to prostitution necessarily stand in any direct proportion to the destitution of his
family. In some communities, people will face death by starvation without
the thought of sacrificing their daughters crossing their minds.[6]

But if the difference does not lie in externals, it must lie in the people
themselves. We are perhaps inclined to say that, at bottom, it concerns a
difference in attitudes. However, this manner of putting it would also be
misleading. For if not seeing bank-robbery as an option is simply regarded
as dependent on a person's attitude, this seems to entail that it is all up to
the individual; that this is a matter on which different opinions may be held.
However, if someone were to suggest bank-robbery as a possible solution
and I became convinced that he really meant it, then (apart from some
extreme or desperate situation, perhaps), I would not explain this to myself
by saying that his attitude to bank-robbery was obviously different from my
own. Rather, I might say, for instance, that I do not understand him, or that
his understanding of what he proposed to do is radically deficient. And this
would probably go with a change in my relation to him: I might come to
feel very distant from him, could no longer, perhaps, trust him, or imagine
having him for a friend; I might stop speaking to him or cut down contacts
to a minimum.[7]

The fact that something is not an open possibility for us belongs to the
way we judge about things. The statement 'You can do it if you rob a bank'
does not, in our understanding, entail the statement 'You can do it'. Only in
the context of a shared way of life (of understanding and judging) are certain
things 'objectively possible or impossible'.

The upshot of this is that the issue of what is economically possible is
not itself to be settled in purely economic terms.

---

[6] A closely related point is used to satirical purpose in Jonathan Swift's *Modest Proposal*.
[7] Of course an individual may be tempted to do that which he knows he could never
seriously put forward as an option. This brings out the sense in which a life in crime is
mostly a solitary life. (It also helps us see why the issue of what can be taken seriously is
not psychological.)
I am not saying that there may not be communities in which differences like these might
be differences of attitude or opinion; however, those communities would be very different
from ours, meaning by 'ours' a community in which such matters are not discussed. In
other words, in such a community, even someone who disapproves of bank-robbery would
think about such things very differently from someone who could not entertain it as an
option. (For an analogous case, consider the disagreements among radical groups in the
1970's between those that 'approved' of political murder and those that did not. Someone
who is prepared to discuss political murder as an option, even if in the end he rejects it,
is closer to someone who is prepared to commit murder than to someone who could not
take such a proposal seriously.

5. Now, in our imaginary argument, the husband, rather than defend his habits by arguing that he could afford them, might simply declare that he was not prepared to give them up. Though admitting that the habits put a strain on their economy, he might deny that they were a luxury, and claim that they were an important part of his life: meeting with friends in the pub, the excitement and the chance of winning small sums of money at the races were part of what, for him, constituted the meaning of life. If there is to be no room for such activities in his life, what point is there in working or in saving money? Rather than things he may or may not be able to afford, we might say, they belong to the things for which allowance has to be made when the issue of what they can afford arises. They might, as it were, belong to the necessities by which he defines himself: in order to give them up, he would have to change.

It is important to be clear about the nature of such a line of defence. We are strongly inclined, I believe, to relativize it, that is, to reduce it to a different though apparently similar type of argument: that of invoking the beneficial effects of a habit, or the detrimental effects of giving it up. Thus, the husband might say that going to the pub is an important way of relaxing after the strains of his day at the office, that he might get physically ill if he had to give it up, etc. Such arguments too are undoubtedly in place on occasion, but I believe it important to resist the tendency to reduce the previous type of argument to these. It is one thing to say that meeting with friends at the pub is important and to refuse to give it up, and quite another thing to say that it is beneficial. The former argument can, in principle, stand on its own, without the support of the latter.[8]

The temptation to relativize arguments in this way can perhaps be understood by considering the dynamics of the discussion. Unlike the kinds of option that will not be seriously considered, the necessity being invoked here is personal. Betting on horses is something people may or may not choose to do. Hence it is open to the wife to accept her husband's stance or to reject it. Its only protection, as it were, is the husband's determination to defend it. Because of this, the temptation will be great for him to try to raise it, as it were, to a higher level of necessity: to transform it to a matter of health, of shared interest or the like, thus placing it beyond questioning.[9]

---

[8] Of course, it is, again, quite a different matter to invoke one's *inability* to give up a habit, though agreeing, say, that it is pointless and maybe even harmful. Here one would be confessing a weakness. But to call a habit important is to reject the idea that it might be considered a weakness. Of course, others may not agree.

[9] We might compare the husband's situation to that of fundamentalist religion in a secularized society. In earlier periods appeals to the Bible or the Koran were automatically considered authoritative. There might have been controversy on how to interpret them, but

Of course, the line between things that are open to discussion and things that are not is not fixed and unambiguous, but is itself to an important extent subject to controversy. It is in connection with such controversy, I would contend, that appeals to morality or conscience are primarily made.[10]

6. The wife's criticism might have quite a different point, however. She might think that by spending his time at the pub, getting drunk, etc., her husband was *wasting his life*. Drinking with friends, she may think, uses up time and strength that should be given to more valuable pursuits.

Now suppose the husband were to defend his habit by saying that he *could afford* wasting his life. Would this be intelligible, except perhaps as an arrogant joke? Wasting one's life is clearly a different matter than squandering opportunities that might have been turned to good use *in* one's life. The waste involved in wasting one's life is not to be spelled out in terms of some goal that one fails to reach. If that were so, one could indeed afford to waste a lot of opportunities, provided one could be assured that there were plenty of more opportunities ahead. However, in speaking of wasting one's life, the risk of waste would be the greater, the more opportunities one had. Thus, a person's realization that she had some special talent, that she lived in fortunate circumstances, was in good health, etc. might give her a heightened sense of obligation. For many people, such a view of life and what it would mean to risk wasting it would be connected with regarding life as a task or as a gift that is not to be used lightly.

The idea that life may be regarded as a task or as a gift may be in need of a comment. It does not require a religious frame of reference in order to

openly flaunting, say, the Ten Commandments was unthinkable. When this situation no longer obtains, the authority of holy texts is seen to be dependent on the determination of those who would uphold it. Fundamentalism today, then, paradoxically, becomes a matter of voluntary submission. A natural response in this situation is for the fundamentalists to turn fanatic, to dig in their spiritual heels, as it were. However, the fact that the status of religious argument in a secularized society is different from its status in a devout society cannot be overcome by an act of will. This is the tragedy of fundamentalism. (Of course, unlike the husband, the fundamentalist cannot invoke the beneficial effects of his creed without betraying the cause itself.)

[10]This may help us appraise the point sometimes made (whether approvingly or not), according to which there can be no morality in business. I believe such a claim can only be understood if it is taken as expressing a reaction to a moral appeal made in connection with some matter of controversy. The point becomes pure nonsense if it is taken to mean that there are literally no limits to the options that a business man will consider. In fact, if the claim were true in this sense – if there were no form of deception, robbery, sabotage, etc, that businessmen were not prepared even to consider, – then, to put it bluntly, there would be no such thing as business life in the first place.

be intelligible.[11] The words 'task' and 'gift', I want to suggest, are being used here in what has been called a secondary sense (on this notion, cf. for instance Cora Diamond (1991)), that is, in the absence of some of the features of their ordinary grammar. Thus, when life is spoken of as a gift, this is not necessarily tied to the notion of a giver, nor, strictly speaking, that of a recipient (after all, the human being who receives the gift of life only comes into being through the gift). Similarly, regarding one's life as a task does not presuppose that there could be a specification of what is involved in the task, nor can the task be regarded as something that could conceivably be completed at some point in time; that would mean, for instance, that one might get through the task before the end of one's life. (On this, cp. Gaita (1991, Chap. 12).) Someone's relating to her life as a task is not something that will show itself in her doing this rather than that, but in the spirit in which she does whatever she does, although her idea of the task will be internally connected with what she considers important or valuable in life. (This means that each person must ultimately decide for herself the nature of the task life sets her.)

When someone comes to think that she has wasted her life, there is no room for the thought that she could afford the waste, nor the thought that the waste could be compensated for. Such considerations go with a way of speaking about waste which connects it with the attainment of some independently identifiable goal. Since there is no such goal in this connection, this is a form of waste that is irreparable.

The idea of irreparable waste may enter into other contexts too; say, into the way we think about the destruction of an important work of art or some historic building; or, again, about the destruction of some tract of wilderness that human beings have imbued with meaning, or about the endangerment of some beautiful species of plant or animal (not, I believe, *any* species). Our regarding some forms of waste as irreparable is an expression of the fact that some things are of ultimate importance for us.

7. The prevalence of economic forms of thought of which I spoke at the outset does not consist solely in the fact that we tend to give economic considerations a dominant role in our decisions, as far as we do. At least in the present connection it is even more important to recognize our inclination to misconstrue our own thoughts and motives by giving an economic interpretation to considerations that are not, in fact, to be understood in

---

[11]It could perhaps be said that the ability to relate to one's life as a gift or a task may help one understand what would be involved in a religious view of life, rather than the other way round.

economic terms. In short, I would argue that even in our culture, the range
of application of purely economic explanations of action is far more limited
than we may be inclined to think. I hope the discussion of uses of the word
'waste' has helped illuminate this point. Among the uses we discussed, that
involving cost-efficiency was apparently the only one that could be spelled
out in more or less purely economic terms.

The inclination to give our motives an economic interpretation is apparently connected with a deeply entrenched view of human action and rationality. On this view, our ability to deliberate and to act rationally presupposes
that the world in which we act is already rationally articulated. The agent
finds herself faced with a range of alternative actions, each of them bound
up with a set of (more or less probable) consequences to which a (more or
less definite) utility function is assigned. Those utility functions may either
be thought of as reflecting some identifiable human needs, or, more subjec-
tively, as being determined by the freely formed preferences of individuals.[12]
Putting my criticism of this view of human action in its most general terms,
I would argue that the world in which we act is, on the contrary, *given* its
articulation in the ways in which we act and respond to the actions of others. Thus, we do not find certain things necessary or exclude other things
from consideration because we have certain needs or wishes, but rather, our
understanding of our own needs and wishes is shaped by the things that we
find necessary or that we exclude from consideration.

---

[12]To what extent the prevalence of economic activity in our culture has contributed
to shaping this view of human action, and to what extent this understanding of human
action, on the other hand, has helped pave the way for an economic culture can only, I
believe, be a matter for speculation.

7 Soul and land

Jakob Meløe [1]

1.   Whatever culture is, it is not nature. Culture is that which is distinct from nature. That is the fundamental contrast in which the concept of culture is set – at least in our culture.

> Apples and pears
> grow on trees
> when they get ripe
> then they fall down.

That is an old children's rule about nature. But if we pick the apples just before they fall on the ground, we interfere ever so slightly with the course of nature – for our own good and without any harm to nature. This, perhaps, is one of the points at which culture borders on nature. Then we store the apples so they will keep until Christmas or New Year. We do something now, four months before Christmas, with a view to Christmas. While we are harvesting the apples, the squirrel is harvesting nuts and storing them up for winter. And we could well say 'with a view to winter'. But maybe not 'with a view to Christmas'. There is little to suggest that the squirrel makes a distinction between Christmas Eve and other days of winter. Here it is what we have in view, Christmas Eve, rather than the length of the view, that makes the storing culture. As well as the way we store the apples, say, indoors and, say, in a different room than the potatoes.

On Christmas Eve mother puts the apples on a dish and passes it around, first to the eldest and then by turns to the youngest, or the other way round. That is culture. The eldest first is one culture, the youngest first another. These are two different cultures within one culture. (We can see why cultures cannot be counted.) But the gift lies at the core of both of them.

---

[1] Translated from Norwegian by Lars Hertzberg.

2. But when mother gives each of the other family members an apple as a gift, does she not give to each of them that which they had already received as a gift of nature when they harvested the apples? Or did she make the apples her own by storing them? There may be a rich pattern in the simple apple ceremony. The pattern may, for instance, be this: The gifts of nature, in this case the apples, do not go to us, but to the master, who has, say, planted the apple trees. (Thus when the children water the apple trees, this does not make them fellow owners. It only counts as helping father, or only as obeying him.) He gives mother the apples, as a gift. She stores them so as to have something to give away. On Christmas Eve mother gives an apple to each of the guests at the family celebration, including father who now receives from her as a gift one of the gifts he gave her last autumn. Or the pattern may be completely different. Father may not have given mother the apples, but may simply have asked her to store them, as his servant, and then to hand them around, as his servant, i.e. as his gift to the person to whom she hands an apple. Or he may be the servant. Or the two of them may in some sense be one, rather than two as in my stories, say, as far as managing the gifts of nature is concerned. The pattern may also be indeterminate between all these stories and some others. (The apple ceremony is like a language game. We see that several worlds may hide in what looks like one and the same language game.)

But whatever pattern the gift is woven into, the gift itself must be there before you can give it away. The gift must be there as a thing, and the thing must be yours, before you can give it away as a gift. It is hard to give things away empty-handed. And the things we acquire, for gifts or for barter, or for ourselves, we either get ready- made from nature, or we get the stuff (the raw materials) for them from nature. In that sense our dealings with nature, say the fact that we can harvest her or get raw materials from her, is basic to our relation to other people. If the apples are not there or if they are not ours, we have no apples to give away as a gift. And in my story the apples are mine because the apple trees are, and the apple trees are mine because I have planted them in my land.

3. But my land, the land I own or have a right to cultivate, is not mine unless others accept it as mine. Relations between people go deep into our relations with nature, into who can harvest what, who can extract raw materials where, etc. This does not mean that the relation between people is more basic than the relation to nature. But it means that the relations between people which order our relation to nature, what we can harvest, what raw materials we can extract, etc, is basic to other relations between people.

Even love between two lovers dies if the lovers die, from starvation, cold, etc. An essential part of love between two people is the division of labour between them. She bakes the bread and he brings the fish ashore. Or the other way round. (When it is the other way round, it is nearly always an exception. But that is a different story.)

Here in Northern Norway we harvest the sea, then the earth and the forest, and the highlands with their lichen and heather. We harvest the sea and the land and we get the material from the forest, for houses and boats. The large trees give us boards for the houses and for the boats, and the smaller trees give us firewood – provided we have the tools. And we could get far with only axe and knife. We built as good boats here in the north before we had saws as after getting them.

First we let the goats eat in the forest and we gathered fodder for the winter wherever we could. Then we drained the marshes, when we had the tools to do so, made fields, made hay and got winter fodder for cattle and goats as well as sheep. In the field we worked on nature in order to remould it into a more yielding nature. There is both skilled work and a long view in a good field. Therefore the field is both culture and nature. In gathering in the hay we gather the fruits of the culture nature we have created in the field.

4. Haymaking is both work and celebration. Those who ordinarily row fishing boats now cut swathes of hay with scythes. (Cutting a swathe: If two or more men are to cut a square field, the first one starts out below in the left corner. When he has made five or six strokes, the next one starts out. Etc. They all hold the same rhythm and they do not get in each other's way.) Those who ordinarily work in the cowshed are now in the field, with a rake. The whole family is working and for the whole family to be working is a celebration, at least on the coast and at least for the kids. The smallest kids sit on the haycart and the biggest may be allowed to jump in the haybarn. And the hay-racks are great to hide in. There is harvest porridge and maybe brandy for the grownups.

Haymaking is the great outdoors celebration just as Christmas is the great indoors celebration. Between the two there is thanksgiving for the harvest, but mainly where the crops of the land support the life of the community. (God does not turn the same face on the farming community as on the fishing community.) The church is richly decorated with flowers, and the stairway leading up to the choir is brimming with bushels of potatoes, cabbage, carrots, turnips, red currants, black currants, and whatever other crops the soil yields in that area. It is a church service in joy over the good gifts of the earth, or the good gifts of God as we also say, since a gift should by rights have a giver. Our joy over the gifts is our thanks to the giver. (If the harvest has been poor, we give thanks all the same. And worry about making up for what is missing.)

Here the church holds a service that springs from our relation to nature. Even if a great deal of work goes into a head of cabbage or a bunch of carrots, starting perhaps with the draining of the marsh, we know that our work did not create the cabbage or the carrot. That is why they are gifts and that is why we give thanks.

A harvest thanksgiving grows naturally from the lives of people where the crops of the soil support that life, whether in Målselv, in Samaria or in Chaldea. But Christmas Eve is a different matter. It is also a time of thanksgiving, in which we give thanks for God becoming man. It is a story that may grip us deeply, but it does not grow naturally out of people's lives whether in Målselv (with its farming and its forestry) or in Lofoten (with its fishing villages). It has reached us from elsewhere, and perhaps we have to understand another culture well before we can understand its deeper meaning. Many of us, or maybe not so many, derive their nourishment from the Old and the New Testament, and maybe understand the deep significance of Christmas. But all the same we celebrate Christmas, most of us do, and put our soul into it, as well as we understand Christmas and the soul.

But haymaking is also a feast or a celebration whether we make it part of harvest thanksgiving or not. Today there are not so many children who can see the grownup men cut strings through the timothy. But even though the mowing machine has removed a rhythm, the making of hay-racks remains, and the promise to be allowed to sit on the haycart, the harvest porridge, the family gathered around the food basket between the hay-racks, etc.

5. But is haymaking a celebration? Is it not enough to say that haymaking is so many workdays for gathering fodder for the cattle for winter, so that we can then get so many liters of milk from them, at a price of so many crowns a liter? For it is all about money, the money we earn selling milk and the money we save by not buying the milk we need for ourselves. And we have had money in view the whole time, through all our calculations, from the time when we first drained the marsh until now when we figure out running and maintenance costs for the tractor and the milking machine. Etc.

The story may be told thus. And we can write out the calculations and put in figures so that we get a true story of incomes and costs. But it is false as a story about what it means to be a human being on earth or as a story about why we do what we do.

We cannot get by without working, and the classical form of work along the coast of Northern Norway is done in the boat and in the cowshed all year round, and in the hayfield in summer. But the fact that we cannot get by without working can be read in two ways, in both of which it is true. On one way of reading it, it tells us that unless we work we will have neither food to eat nor a roof over our heads. Not since the Garden of Eden. The other way of reading it tells us that it is good for a man or a woman to work (that we fare ill, as human beings, from not working). We have hands for working, eyes for seeing, a head for thinking, etc. Our constitution is such that we need boats for getting out to sea to catch fish. Up here in the north we need houses and heating to get by. Etc. But our constitution is also such that what we have to do because of our constitution and because we are here, we also have to do in order to flourish as human beings. That is why it is good to do what we need our hands, eyes, head, language, each other, etc., in order to do. That is why it does us good to build boats, to row for fish, to build houses, bake bread, weave mats, to play with children, to teach the children to row, to bake, to weave, etc., to tell each other what we have seen or learnt, each in our corner of the world, to write letters about it, etc. And it does us good to do so with the skill we gradually acquire through experience.

If we are made for thinking, we are perhaps also made for counting, doing calculations, etc. And the concepts of economics get their human connection through farming, fishing, handicrafts, and other good forms of human life. But if we make economic calculations *the* story of why we do what we do, of what it is to be human, we lose our understanding both of ourselves and of others. The very point of making an occasional calculation also gets lost.

If we are to describe life on a farm, accounting belongs there. But the place of haymaking in the life on the farm is not its place in the accounts. The true story of haymaking can only be told in the light of a true understanding of what a human life is, or the other way round. And when a true account is given of haymaking, we see that it can spring forth as a celebration, in our joy over nature and each other. That is what haymaking is like, even if now and then it is not like that.

8   Music and the frailness of wonder

(Contemporary music as an expression of a technological understanding of being)

Hannes Nykänen

How are economic values reflected in contemporary art music? There is an inclination to think that there must be a rather direct connection here, that there is something that could be identified as 'the commercial features' in music. I doubt whether anything interesting could be brought into view by this way of putting the problem. This is because, firstly, I see no reason to suppose that composers would generally be insincere and speculate about whatever is commercially rewarding. Secondly, even to the extent this would be the case the music cannot be described in economic terms. Instead we must say that music is simplistic, sentimental, and the like. We must in other words go beyond economic terms.

Thirdly, and this is a more general form of the earlier points, money is a seduction that we are familiar with. What perplexes us today, however, is not anything like greediness. Rather, we want to understand why economic motives announce themselves so readily. The question could perhaps be formulated like this: 'Why have economic values acquired such a weight?' This question indicates that we are looking for something that is not itself of economical nature. My suggestion is that the centrality of economical values depends-on something I will call the 'technological understanding of being'.

'The technological understanding of being' denotes a cluster of *essentially* interrelated capacities and attitudes; (i) the power resting in science and technology to intervene in the world and (ii) the inclination in politics to give priority to rights instead of obligations. These two features combine in a general attitude characterized by 'demand'. 'Demand' implies the idea that difficulties in life are seen as *problems*, that is, as something that can be brought in accord with our demand and thus; *solved*. This sort of demand presupposes an ability to intervene in the world and such is supplied by science and technology.

To describe the technological understanding of being is to describe the essence of technology. To accept the concept 'essence of technology' is to accept that technology is not merely an instrument we use but that the use of (scientifically grounded) technology is connected with a morally related outlook on things. 'The essence of technology' in other words is about the way technology affects our deepest ideas about what *ought to be*.

The opposite to the technological understanding of being is to wonder at the existence of things, to see sacredness in them. This sacredness transcends the idea of nature as an object of human interest and evaluation. Sacredness is not a value. It can be *seen* by human beings only but when it is seen, it is seen as something that is independent of human evaluations.

This sacredness can only be where the wonder addresses itself towards all that is given and not only towards human beings. If only man is something to wonder at then wonder is conditional which means that it is founded on criteria and qualities. In this case 'wonder' has already ceased to be. 'Admiration of man' has taken its place. By the same token 'sacredness' has vanished in the face of a plurality of values. (What I say does not imply that things in nature and man should be considered in an equal manner. The respect which is a part of wonder has a different content in connection with human beings than with things in nature.)

The problems of our time cannot be understood in the terms of philosophy of value since this kind of thinking is part of the problems. The technological understanding of being is supplying the frames for philosophy of value; to value something is to *ascribe* significance to it. Judgements of value are open to consent and dissent, they are relative. By the same token they are dependent on criteria and adjustable by way of argument. And so moral calculation with value-parameters is thought to maximize the variety of demands.

But whatever is relative cannot escape the fact that it is grounded in some ideas that are *unquestioned*. These ideas might be called metaphysical. In this chapter they will be called essential since they make up our ideas about what things *are*. When moral and aesthetic matters are considered to be about value, and by the same token relative, this stems from an idea about what these matters flare. (This is not to claim that the use of the word 'value' would automatically be relativistic. This is not how language works. 'Absolute value' is fine as long as one remembers that one is then speaking about something that is not dependent on our valuing it. Also, 'absolute value' is not the same as 'infinite value' I might find a work of art infinitely valuable but the way I 'value' my child is not of this order. – 'Value' is originally an economic term and perhaps this fact will make it seem less suitable as an important moral concept, especially to those who do not think that ethics is, in any sense, about 'value- transactions'.)

'Technology' does not refer only to technical devices but to all forms of scientifically grounded organization or to all forms of rational organization of some concrete or non-concrete substance. Thus this term is suitable when speaking about psychological, pedagogical, environmental as well as computational technologies. This is how music enters the picture. Also music has become an instance of rational organization – of sound. But has not music always been such? No. Not *at all*.

What does it mean to say that music has become a rational organization? This is what must be shown. But trying to do this is connected with a number of issues. Firstly, what is the meaning of 'wonder' and how is the technological understanding of being in discord with it? These are the issues of the two first sections. Then, in section three I try to explain what 'wonder' and 'essence of technology' mean in the case of music.

Since I make no historical claims I do not want to give any exact definition of 'contemporary music'. What I have in mind is twentieth century Western art music. 'Tonal music' refers to Western art music up to the beginning of this century and here too I see no point in insisting on exact demarcations. Thus contemporary music that is tonal does not belong under the term 'tonal music'. This might sound strange but I hope it will become clearer later on.

Wonder, essence and quality in relation to saying and showing

It is not necessary to use either the word 'essence' or that of 'being' in order to explore the meaning of wonder. They are used partly because of convenience and partly in order to indicate that some of the ideas that are connected with the use of these words are both important and philosophically legitimate. But these ideas themselves could probably be expressed without using words like 'essence' or 'being'. (This goes for many other words used in philosophy but I will put aside this issue.)

A number of modern thinkers have pointed out the importance of wonder. Wittgenstein formulates it by saying for instance: 'How extraordinary that anything should exist'. (Wittgenstein 1965, 8). In another place he says that when he wonders at the sky it is a matter of irrelevance whether it is blue or cloudy (ibid. 9). I do not think that this means Wittgenstein did not care about the way things look. What it means is, I believe, that his wondering is not conditional. He does not mean that he is struck by the sky only when it has this or that special colour. Rather the sky is always something to wonder at; any colour is a wonder. What Wittgenstein means is probably just the opposite to indifference towards the way things look.

The curious thing is that the expressions of this wonder do not describe anything; they are not founded on any facts whatsoever. This is of course connected with the unconditional character of wonder. Wittgenstein thought (at least at the time of his 'Lecture on ethics') that any effort to describe the wonder is bound to produce nonsense. In fact he thought that all efforts to say something sensible about religion and ethics were fruitless. It seems clear that for Wittgenstein at this time sense, as opposed to nonsense, is to be understood in terms of description; what can be described is sensible and what cannot is nonsense. I shall pass over this idea of nonsense. The word has clearly a very special meaning here and Wittgenstein felt the deepest respect for this sort of 'nonsense'.

What is interesting is the thought that words used to express our wonder are not descriptions of any existing object. The words do not refer to any object with such and such qualities and so, in a sense, nothing is *said*. Instead the words *show* a certain attitude towards things. In another place Wittgenstein says:

> The miracles of nature. One might say: art *shows* us the miracles of nature. It is based on the *concept* of the miracles of nature. (The blossom, just opening out. What is *marvelous* about it?) We say: 'Just look at it opening out!'. (Wittgenstein 1980, 56)

But of course we cannot think that it is only in art that wonder can show itself. Wonder presupposes a language. ('It is based on the *concept* of the miracles of nature'). If words, like works of art, can show the wonder then is not something said too? What is the difference between saying and showing?

It is possible to tell a person, say, the way to his or her hotel room quite unambiguously. Likewise it is possible to tell which point of the compass the window is facing, how big the room is, how many beds it has etc. These facts can be captured in language, they can be *said*. But we cannot *tell* a person how nice the hotel room is in such a way that he could give an aesthetical response. To do this we must *show* him the room. Suppose he likes it very much: 'Oh how...!' His words do not describe the room, they are not qualitative remarks, describing facts, but aesthetical judgements that *show* what he thinks of the room.

Ethical and aesthetical judgements can be transformed into qualities, that is, facts, but then they are no longer ethical nor aesthetical *responses*.

Instead they become descriptions: 'You'll find it; it is a cute little house with a beautiful garden and it lies at the end of the road...'. But this kind of usage presupposes a use where these judgements are not factual, uses where they are judgements in the sense of being aesthetic responses.

There can be no facts in language if we are not first *struck* by something; we do not first state facts and then check whether they are important or not. Something must be *worthy* of being a fact. Things must first *show* themselves in language before they can be stated as facts in it: Prior to facts there must be words ('fact' cannot, logically speaking, be the first of words). Initially then words show what things are ('to us' if you like) which amounts to letting things *be at all.*

If language consisted merely in description, in that which can be said, then there would be nothing that shows *how* we understand things. We would merely be dealing with them and in a sense things would be simply instruments and language would be only communication. Why? Consider the following example: Dolphins have a complicated system of communication. But no matter how intricate this system might be, there is nothing that indicates that we have language here. Probably dolphins communicate in a more sophisticated way than other animals. But is there anything that could show that the way dolphins communicate is different in *kind,* and not only in degree, from the communication systems of other animals? The complexity of their communication cannot do this. What *could?*

Now, what if dolphins had some sort of funeral ceremony? And what if they decorated things, forbade and punished certain kinds of behaviour, had a 'silent moment' before eating their food etc.? To imagine such things makes it impossible to really think of dolphins as *dolphins.* They seem more like men. (I owe this point to Lars Hertzberg.) In terms of what can be described, *said,* these 'aesthetic' and 'moral' features would however add nothing; they would not increase the complexity of the communication system since all the words used in aesthetic and moral contexts could already exist as purely descriptive words (in a similar manner as 'beauty' could be about sexual preferences and 'goodness' about sympathetic behaviour). Still, morals and aesthetics are connected with attitudes and responses that amount to nothing less than changing, in our example, the communication system into a *language* – and so dolphins into human beings. What has appeared, in addition to mere communication, is a stance towards the things that are. This stance contains concepts like wonder, gratitude, respect, beauty and awe. Only when these kinds of responses can be expressed do things really come into being.

Wonder is about being and it is expressed not as something that can be said in words but as something that *shows* our attitude and understanding. These are fundamental features that characterize language and, by the same

token, human beings. As Wittgenstein puts it: 'The correct expression for
the wondering at the existence of the world is no sentence in language. The
correct expression is the existence of language itself.' (Wittgenstein 1965,
11).

There could be no language if we did not respond to things in similar
ways; that is, if we did not find things to be important in similar ways. The
existence of words *show* that we have similar responses and that we thus
agree about the *essence* of things.

Things can *be*, have essences, only in an ethical understanding. To agree
in language is to *have* such an understanding. When things have an essence
they are understood ethically; to show something in language is connected
with being struck by a wonder. What is shown is the essence.

Essences are about that which is shown. Therefore one cannot ask what
the qualities are that make up the essence of something. To say, for instance,
that the essence of the apple is made up by certain characteristic qualities is
a confusion.

Simon Weil points out that to say to someone 'I am not interested in your
person' is not an offense while the statement 'I am not interested in you' is
as bad as can be (Weil 1986, 70). I would suggest that the first statement
is only about descriptive issues, about that which can be said. The second
statement is connected with that which is essential though it is a denial of it.
It is as if the offense would contain an effort to disconnect a person from the
realm of wonder. – There is an asymmetry between description and essence.
To be interested in descriptive aspects of a person, of his personality, does
not entail that one in any sense respects or loves him. On the other hand
respect and love are always tied to a person and so entail an interest in the
personality.

Suppose that two persons are completely in agreement about the description of a third person. Still it is possible that one of the two thinks this person
is indifferent while the other one loves him. Suppose on the other hand that
two persons both loved a third one but that their descriptions of him would
be contradictory. Would we not think that one of them is confused about
the essence of the beloved one? And would not the love then be a confused
one too?

What is essential is not only a response irrespective of what is understood.
Essence presupposes a correct description but it cannot be reduced to such
a description.

When words *show* things then they are about the essence of things, about
what things are. As has been said; if there were no agreement about what
things are we could have no language. The more factual, non-essential, the
aspects that are thought to be sufficient for meaning the less agreement

you will have. Things will become analogical to the facts that, empirically or functionally, can be predicated about them, they will be *functional complexes*. This is another way of saying that the meaning of language (and consequently, understanding between people) is breaking down.

If the meaning of a word is constituted only by correct uses then the word loses what is important in its meaning. All we can say is: 'This use is as correct as that one'. Another way of saying this would be that the grammar of the word 'important' (hinting at what is essential) is lost.

When things become functional complexes this means that the meaning of the words we use in connection with them is constituted by correct uses. 'Correct uses' again correspond to correct descriptions: if we say 'A is in love with B' then this is supposed to be a *correct use* of 'love' if it corresponds to a certain description of the relationship. Here the meaning of 'love' is constituted by facts. Whether what A feels is *really* love does not here seem to be a question about the meaning of the word (it is used correctly) but about morals (whatever could be meant by that in *this* view).

But the meaning of 'love' (what love *is*) is the same as that which it *should* be. Is not the meaning of most words really dependent on what should be the case rather than on instances that *can merely be identified* by words? If one accepts this, then it means that correct use as such is *not* the determining ground for what love is; all uses are not compatible with what love should be – and is. The fact that we have the word 'love' shows that we agree about the essence of love. To take *actual* uses (to the extent they are correct as a determining ground for the meaning of 'love') is to break down the meaning of the word.

Things can be, have essences, only in an ethical understanding. To agree in language is to *have* such an understanding. When things have an essence they are understood ethically; to *show* something in language is connected with wondering at the existence of the world. What is shown is the essence.

Wondering at the world is not some sort of passive gaping. It is connected with an attitude which lies at the core of our morality, namely *respect*. One cannot talk of respect without wonder being a part of it. 'Respect' means something more than 'acknowledging the rights of others', more than acknowledging, so to speak, that my neighbour too counts as one when issues are settled. When respect has its source in wonder then this means that '*obligation*' is a part of this understanding.

If wonder is not part of obligations then these are only about obeying rules. Wonder which is not connected with an understanding of the obligations that spring from it, is only a mixture of a particular kind of aestheticism and sentimentality.

Many philosophers would probably claim that the philosophical centrality of ideas connected with 'essence' vanished because these ideas have been proved to be faulty. Of course I do not deny that there were many problems, for instance, in the medieval doctrines of essentials. But this was hardly the reason for discarding them. Rather, I believe, they vanished because the absolute and ethical outlook on the universe lost its importance. (Frederick Copleston seems to confirm this when he contrasts St. Thomas and Ockham: "Ockham [...] discarded [St. Thomas's] theory of divine ideas. The consequence was that for him the similarities which gave rise to universal concepts are simply similarities, so to speak, of fact [.]" (Copleston 1985, 58, vol III))

What I have tried to show is that wonder lies at the heart of our language and, by the same token, of our morality. This amounts to saying that our humanity springs from wonder; seeing *as* a miracle that something exists in the first place and feeling gratitude for this being so.

The technological imperative and 'demand'

The essence of technology does not refer to any qualitative denominator supposed to be common to all technology, science and rational organization in general. There are no common features of this kind. Instead, the essence of technology is about those features in modern life that alienate us from the moral conception that is connected with wonder. But there is no necessary condition that makes these instances incompatible with wonder. In a strict, conceptual sense science and technology have no bearing on issues outside their field (such as moral, religious and aesthetic issues). This insight, however, is not one that science or even philosophy teaches us. It is part of an idea about what, on the one hand, science *should* be and on the other hand what ethics and religion *should* be. It is precisely this idea which is falling apart in the technological understanding of being. In this latter case science is thought to be relevant to every kind of issue. But this understanding is of course not scientific in itself. It also expresses an idea about what science *should* be. This 'should' expresses the essence of technology.

Consider the following statement by I.C. Jarvie:

> [T]he *rationality of science* is not exhausted by the *practices of science* – why else is there a continuing methodological debate? Yet the paradigm of rationality is action taken with full knowledge; the paradigm of full knowledge is scientific knowledge; therefore action taken to gain scientific knowledge is at the heart of any idea of rationality. (Jarvie 1970, 269)

'Action' is central to Jarvie's idea. This also shows itself when he, arguing against Peter Winch, would like to prove the superiority of our knowledge, as against that of the Azande, by referring to what kind of things we can *do* better than the Azande (ibid. 264). 'Rationality' is 'action taken with full knowledge'. This can mean nothing else than that this is what Jarvie thinks 'rationality' *should* mean. It should be about *action* and not for instance about 'contemplation'.

This is not, I think, merely Jarvie's personal opinion. A characteristic feature of modern science is not only that it gives us a description of the workings of nature. Science also aims at showing how nature works by way of reproducing events in nature. This is how modern science differs from 'systematic observation' and speculative explanation. (Though speculation seems to be back again. But this is a different issue.)

Consider the work of an evolutionary biologist. Is he only trying to recapitulate what happened long ago by studying fossils? If this were the only thing that his science was about he might as well be said to study the temporal order of creation. But he most certainly is not. Why? It belongs to his field of research to find a mechanism which will show that things really go the way he claims they do. He, personally, need not be occupied with this but the search for a mechanism is what makes his work science as opposed to a 'story about the past'. To find a mechanism means ultimately that science must be able to put it to work. (For instance the physico-chemical mechanism that creates amino acids, the building stones of life, is constantly searched for.) What in the end defines any science is the urge to gain control of things, to show how they work.

(It seems that astronomy cannot demonstrate its theories. Still, if astronomy did not have intimate relations to the mechanisms that for instance quantum physics has demonstrated it would be a completely different science. More generally: The urge to control mechanisms cannot be understood only in terms of specific demonstrations in specific cases. This urge determines the whole essence of science. What can and cannot be demonstrated in astronomy is an *open* question. If it was a closed one such that no demonstration was possible then astronomy would be a wholly descriptive science and radically different from what it is now.)

The relationship between the experimental set-up and nature is mostly problematic; the conditions created in experiments are seldom found in nature. (For more on this see Ian Hacking (1983).) Experiments then show what can be shown by 'purified' and controlled arrangements. I think this dimension of control is crucially important with regard to the way science influences our understanding of being. I shall leave aside the problems concerning scientific realism and the nature of the truth of scientific theories. What is undeniable is that science shows what it is to control nature and in this respect it is essentially technological.

If technological control in science were only about showing how nature works then science would still be an activity completely different from what it actually is. In this case science could be something like a display of nature in the way clocks were first built to display the celestial harmony. But the technological Control also means 'control' in the sense: capacity to *use* science and technology in order to solve practical problems. These practices are powerful tools for making our projects possible and for finding new possibilities for acting. To do this we must understand nature as a resource (cf. Heidegger (1962)) and as a mechanism to be controlled. This is one aspect of the demand mentioned in the beginning of this chapter. Now I will say a few words about another aspect.

The concept of obligation is connected with that of wonder. This is not the case with the concept of rights when it is thought of in the spirit of enlightenment. (Here I am indebted to Simone Weil, see Weil (1986, 105-140).) The concept of rights refers to those things that a person can legitimately, or so it is assumed, *demand.* When this idea is accepted as the foundation of society then it will lead to a situation where politics is about distributing the legitimate demands of citizens in a just way. Since rights and not obligations are the issue this distribution will take on an utilitarian form: 'If these measures are taken it will beneficial for the greatest number of people.' And, further, since rights in many cases presuppose economical resources (like the right to education) the utilitarian distribution will most often be about money. This conception of rights constitutes the other aspect of demand.

These two aspects of demand are conjoined in a singular view and what we have here is a way of thinking, of understanding being, that shows itself in all areas of our culture. Ian Hacking has showed how a calculative way of thinking, in the form of probability and statistics, is connected with efforts to control society. He shows that the emergence of chance and indeterminism does not enhance freedom (nor chaos):

> There is a seeming paradox: the more the indeterminism, the more the control. This is obvious in the physical sciences. Quantum physics takes for granted that nature is at bottom irreducibly stochastic. Precisely that discovery has immeasurably enhanced our ability to interfere with and alter the course of nature. A moment's reflection shows that a similar statement may be attempted in connection with people. The parallel was noticed quite early. Wilhelm Wundt, one of the founding fathers of quantitative psychology, wrote as early as 1862: 'It is statistics that

first demonstrated that love follows psychological laws.' (Hacking 1990, 2)

Hacking shows how this 'taming of chance' is connected with an urge to control all areas of society, also ethics: "No public decision, no risk analysis, no environmental impact, no military strategy can be conducted without decision theory couched in terms of probabilities. By covering opinion with a veneer of objectivity, we replace judgement by computation" (ibid. 4). Here we see how the 'distribution of demands' uses methods (scientific rationality) which also are expressions of demand. This of course is no coincidence. Weil (1986, 106) points out that rights are, really, only the objective form of obligations. (What are obligations for me as a subject are rights for my neighbour seen as an object.) When rights have been taken as a foundation of the modern society this means that a strange reversal has taken place: what was my duty towards others has become a right that I can demand from others. This has been of consequence.

Obligations can never become immoderate whereas the concept of rights give us no shield against immoderation. The claims to rights can be harmonized only through calculation and comparison. And if this is to be done as exactly and impartially as possible should we not use, where possible, scientific rationality? It must be noted that the concept of rights does not offer us any grounds for judging the justness of the distribution of rights – what one has a right to is precisely the issue. (Obligations do not either offer us any grounds for judging their 'application' but, as noted, immoderation is no danger here.) This means that the distribution of rights must be done according to principles *external to* the rights themselves. Rights are only, so to speak, parameters in the calculus. Rights are also merely subjective wishes and they are of interest insofar as they are statistically significant – 'normal'. This means that the moral discussion in a society cannot be carried out in terms of the substantial goodness (that rights are supposed to be about) but in terms of something external, namely principles of distribution or: utilitarian 'ethics'.

Imagine, by contrast, a society where obligations are fundamental. There would probably be just as many problems with injustice in this society as in any other. But the problems would be discussed in terms internal to ethics; 'Can one say that the person in authority has fulfilled his duties towards these people?', 'What are his duties in this case?' 'Did he neglect his duty by simply obeying his superior?' etc. The issue is about what, morally speaking, should be done, not about what it is reasonable to demand.

When technology has acquired an essential role in society it means that the concept of 'problem' is understood in a certain way. 'Problem' indicates that there is some phenomenon we do not yet master scientifically and technically. To solve the problem is to learn how to master the phenomenon; and to master it means that the phenomenon can be made an instrument of our will. That is; to solve a problem is to increase our power to will. 'Problem' means that there is something that we cannot yet make obey our will. This kind of willing, which I have called demand, presupposes an externally related method as its instrument, or; the essence of technology (in the broad sense) is demand. By contrast, a moral understanding is about internal relationships. Here the problem is about seeing how to get *oneself* in accord with things, or how to keep away from others, or when and how to face difficulties etc. All this presupposes an effort to *understand* things and, in a sense, to *obey* their essence (this is what 'internal' means). Nowhere do we find the attitude to *make* something yield *our* will (this is the external force).

Of course the idea of obeying, which is at the heart of obligations and morality in general, is not ruled out today. But it seems as if most instances of 'action taken with full knowledge' are put to work in order to satisfy our 'legitimate' demands (rights). And then problems and their solutions look the way described. This is not, however, merely a moral confusion. It is also an 'ideal'; we have the *right* to demand certain things. What things? Well, those things that *can* be demanded and that make our lives easier and more comfortable. The wish for comfort is very closely connected with technology (for more on this see Ellul (1965, 66)). Technology is precisely about serving us with *easy* solutions *and* about finding new possibilities for demanding things. We need no longer *dream* about things, just wait and see if they will be available during our lifetime. (Or, as Bloch puts it, we live in a time when the Utopia can be made come true.) The things that can be demanded can be expressed in terms of a technological imperative: if something *can* be done then it *has* to be done. It is part of this imperative to find applications that will be available to as many people as possible (to make the applications as non-exclusive as possible). This interest lies in the spirit of rights as well as in that of progress – and in the spirit of commercialism.

Now, what can be done has to be done because what can be demanded is that which *can be done*. A current example: If science can overcome sterility then one can demand the right to have children – and maybe soon: children with certain qualities.

Wonder is connected with obligations, that is, with a moral understanding of things. The concept of rights is connected with an external method of distribution. This combination is called the technological understanding of being. The things in the world cannot here be seen in the light of wonder but rather as something to be *controlled* so they can become part of our utopia of demand.

Here I will end my description of the technological understanding. The description is perhaps fragmentary but hopefully still to the point. It seems to conform with many other views on technology and modernity. There is however one possible objection on a very general level that should be considered. It might be said that the description of the two ways of understanding being does not allow for enough precision in the distinction. With reference to Habermas it might be pointed out that the distinction between 'system-rationality' and 'communicative rationality' is lost. The latter, according to Habermas's theory, is a human resource with the potentiality of breaking the pre-dominance of the former.

Habermas's ideas exemplify the problem they seek to solve, namely the external method: the idea of a saving faculty ('communicative rationality') which is itself external to the problems we face. More importantly, if one thinks that there is some specific sort of rationality or technology that could steer us clear of the terrors of 'system-rationality', then how does one know, if this saving rationality cannot be described, that not also this saver is imbued with the bad rationality? If, on the other hand, the saver can be described then we need not speak about it in the abstract as some *kind* of rationality. Instead we can look and see if the idea is helpful or not.

Any idea that describes the problems of modernity in external terms only ('instrumental reason', 'reification', 'logocentrism' etc.) makes the problems incomprehensible and is an instance of the problem itself. (This goes as well for the efforts of *explaining* our situation by drawing conclusions from the history of ideas.) The disaster of our time is precisely this, that if there is a problem then we think that (i) it *has to be* solved. The implication here is that (ii) our demand is the sole determining ground; the ideal solution is the one which gives us precisely what we demanded. From this it follows that (iii) the problem cannot be comprehended by contemplating the situation at hand. We are not interested in what we should do but in what we can get. And one can never know what method is most efficient in fulfilling a demand. The method is thus by necessity external to moral understanding. The general tendency to understand things in terms of external relationships springs from a moral confusion. This tendency cannot be understood merely as an epistemic conviction.

The efforts to describe modernity in terms of whatever sort of reason offer us a picture where some external force, like a dysfunction in an organism, is causing danger. This force is not reducible to the will of any single individual – anymore than the market forces are. This force is thought to be an infinitely complex result of western metaphysics, religion, science, economics, politics, philosophy and what not. The remedy must of course be equally elusive.

There is some truth in such views; they are instances of the problem at hand. If we think that our problems are caused by some method of thinking and that we need to locate and describe this method in order to steer clear of the problems; if we think this, then these problems do not have anything to do with ethics. We cannot understand the world in moral terms. What the world is, is not dependent on our actions as morally responsible persons but on our actions being a part of a huge mechanism. The problems are external to our understanding. We are only victims of some 'system'. This system must be changed but what really happens is inconceivable in a similar manner as what happens in a computer is inconceivable. These ideas are *expressions of demand*; what is demanded is a solution, that is: a mechanism that can correct the dysfunctions of society in such a way that *we* do not need to start adjusting ourselves (other than in a technical sense: putting waste in two bags instead of one only) – indeed we need not understand anything about the way society is cured. We need only want the cure, then make some small technical adjustments and leave the problem to the experts.

However, the world is what it is because of our moral inclinations, inclinations that belong to each and anyone. This inclination is best described by 'demand'. we see how a moral idea that is *ours* is internally connected with most of the problems we see around us – they become comprehensible. That we can have such a moral idea as expressed by 'demand' depends on our capacity to intervene in the world – on technology. That technology is what it is (not, for instance, a depiction of the eternal harmony nor merely 'the using of tools') depends on this role it has. If this is seen then we will be aware of the fact that we have a tendency and an urge to understand things in a technological way which means that any form of acting and thinking will change in accordance with this understanding (and so Habermas's 'communicative rationality' is technological in essence).

The technological understanding of being has spread over all thought and action. That it can be heard in contemporary music shows this. That it seems difficult to conceive of contemporary music where this understanding would not be heard shows the scope of the problem. If the problems of modernity could be understood in external terms, as some specific sort of rationality that has acquired a dominant position, then it would be impossible to explain why this external force has become so inescapable in an area like music. But if these problems are connected with the way each of us tends to understand being then it becomes perfectly sensible.

Words and music: internal and external relationships

How does music *show* the 'wonders of nature'? And how can it show a technological understanding of things? 'Music is all about sounds.' Or am I going to say that music is capable of representing the technological understanding of being? I will have to say something about words and music.

It is trivial to say that in music practice always precedes theory. This observation can perhaps be connected with another, less trivial one which could go like this: before we can *say* things *about* music there must be words that show what it is.

Music is not a natural phenomenon. In music we show feelings, attitudes, character, ways of understanding things. This is why the words we use when responding to music are not externally related to music (the way the colour of the house is to the fact that the house *is* a house) but internally (the way 'roof' and 'wall' are connected to 'house'). That we *respond to music* is quite inseparable from there being such a response as music is. The words we use (and also gestures, dancing, singing) are not hypotheses about music. These words are, as something shown, necessary to music; if there were no meaning in uttering them this would by the same token mean that there would be no meaning in music – there would be no music.

The kind of response that music is, is constituted by wondering at being. Why? Music is not a way of saying something. If it were, it would be an extremely arbitrary form of saying something (and compared to this even the dolphins seem to do better). If music were about saying something then the importance of it would be wholly inconceivable (we do better with words).

Music, and art in general, is one way of showing one's attitude towards things. And showing, in general, is connected with the very concept of humanity. The showing consists in a response of some kind. (It cannot be merely an intellectual idea.) This response is not the composer's if this is taken to mean that the listener only tries to detect what the composer expresses. (Here music becomes precisely some system of representation.) The music must become a response of the listener too to the extent it is to be music. If music would not be a response of the listener as well as that of the composer and interpreter then music could not be any response at all; for how are we to *know* that music is a response of the composer *only*? If music is no response of *ours* then nothing can be *shown* in and by it.

Musical works (each in their characteristic way) open up a possibility to respond to wonder. What music is, is internally connected with the ways we show our response; playing, singing, dancing, facial expressions, gestures, utterances etc. show what music is and vice versa. What is shown has a distinct character whether or not we find words and sentences that describe it. What then, when we think we *have* found words that 'fit' some piece of music? What is the role of these words? Here we must distinguish between cases where the words we use *show* our response and cases where we try to describe the character of the music.

Consider this analogy: a person is struck by a very humorous but bawdy joke. Someone who hears it might be ashamed and smile shyly while someone else might laugh vulgarly. These responses do not contradict one another. One could even say that these different reactions make the character of the joke clearer. There is no given set of adequate responses to the joke. Still any response is not adequate; someone who smiles sweetly has probably missed the point. If one tries to *describe* the joke then any description that is a description of an adequate response will do. But the joke cannot be exhaustively described in the way we state facts *in* language (saying something) since the joke is constituted by something *shown*.

By analogy, I will call descriptive concepts that are about adequate responses to music 'essential concepts'. Essential concepts constitute the possible meanings of a musical work or a group of works. It is by reference to these concepts that our responses are articulated. This does not mean that we are thinking of certain words when listening to music. It means that certain words are specially relevant when we discuss our understanding of music. Of course it is not settled in advance which words we can use with respect to some work. But the openness of our possible descriptions does not imply that simply any description would do. Insofar as the work has some character our description must be connected with it. When I say that essential concepts constitute the possible meaning in a work I point to the general spirit that some work expresses.

The whole aesthetic use of language is an expression of the essence of musical works (and so is the musical interpretation of them). When we speak about 'climactic modulations', 'contrasting themes', 'masterly counterpoint', 'tragic themes', etc. we on the one hand say things in language (describe them) and on the other hand in doing this we show what sort of importance music has to us (we respond to the wonder). One and the same predicate can be an essential response ('What a tragic theme!') or a description ('I think the theme is tragic rather than melancholy').

As is well known there have been many theories that try to explain the meaning of music in terms of emotion; music is, in some sense or other, the language of emotions. These theories are bound to fail as theories about musical meaning. It is simply untenable to describe music as some sort of language or symbol-system that expresses emotions. In another way: What music is (essentially) cannot be accounted for in qualitative terms. And this is what most theories have attempted to do. Such theories try to *explain* music and so they understand music as something, as it were, *said* in (musical) language. The preoccupation is therefore to find symbolic and semiotic structures in music – and this has clearly failed.

The centrality of emotion cannot, however, be swept aside on these grounds. To deny the importance of emotions would lead to an awkward position since it would imply that almost all people (composers alike) have misjudged music. But it would be better to speak about music as a *human response* than as an expression of emotions. Human responses *show* attitudes, emotions and character and so a way of understanding something.

What I have said so far applies to what I have called 'tonal music'. The important thing is not how readily one might find emotive concepts that are adequate for some tonal work (in the case of J.S. Bach this is not all that easy). The important thing is that this music is (or rather: can, if it is good music, be) connected with a multitude of human responses that are ultimately connected with the wonder of being (and this is all too evident in the case of Bach). I shall not give examples of the way we use words when we express our understanding of what the music shows. I think we are familiar enough with that. Now I shall try to say somethinq about contemporary music.

The essence of contemporary music is such that it is incompatible with any response connected with wonder. There is, for instance, no temptation to call this music a 'language of emotions'. The latter idea, though confused, arises from an awareness of the fact that music is a human response – and a response to the wonder of being. Why is this not the case with contemporary music?

Let me start with a list of concepts that I believe to be, *still today*, of central importance to contemporary music: 'complexity', 'control', 'structure', 'organization', 'material' and 'formal (that is: external) relationship'. These concepts are by their nature externally related to their 'object'. Consider this analogy: When a person shows anger the expressions of this anger are internally connected with what we understand by 'anger' while a description of hormonal states is external to this concept. If we take the latter as an essential description, what anger *really* is, then this shows our ideal. This means that we think external relationships are more important than internal ones and so, in a curious way, we substitute the former for the latter. A similar substitution has occured in music; what is internal, responses to music *and* music *as* response, has become external. 'Organization of sound', something external, has become essential. This means that 'tonality' is now only 'one way of organizing sound' – it is not what it used to be.

The centrality of the above-mentioned concepts ('complexity' etc.) *shows* that they express an aesthetical ideal and in this sense they are internally related, by way of a curious substitution, to music – they are essential. The character of our response to music must be articulated in connection with these concepts. This tells us something about the response. We do not for instance say: 'What marvelous complexity!' 'Complexity' contradicts the spirit of enthusiasm and wonder that is connected with this form of response. There is no question, however, about removing the concept of complexity and saving the enthusiastic response; we *are not* struck by wonder when listening to contemporary music. Our response is in some sense about 'complexity'.

In a technological understanding the concepts listed above are, of course, externally related to one another. 'Complexity' refers to the quantity of relationships, 'control' is some specific tool or method, 'structure' refers to the distribution of elements, 'organization' is some mode of 'putting together' (and its result), 'material' is the sounding stuff used and 'formal relationship' refers to the (formal) qualities of relationships.

By no means do I deny that it might, in *specific* situations, be quite fruitful to look at these concepts separately (ignoring their internal connections for specific purposes). They are surely distinct concepts. But if we understand them as being *essential* then they are internally connected. Now they express an understanding of music which, further, is a part of an understanding of being.

We could very well speak about the structure of a work by Mozart. Also we could point to great complexities in texture, perhaps about his overall control of the design and the character of his thematic material etc. But if we ask what the music is, what kind of understanding it expresses, then these concepts are wholly irrelevant. In the case of Mozart these concepts are externally related to the music (and, consequently, to each other) – they are only specific analytic tools. If we want to touch upon the essence of Mozart's music we must speak in a completely different way.

Now, what does it look like when the concepts in question are seen as expressions of the essence of music and so are internally related? Here 'complexity' does not have the role of an extrinsic, analytic concept (as it had in the case of Mozart); it does not merely describe a quality of texture but is connected with what makes the music important as music. 'Complexity' is quantitative and often it is couched in terms of information theory. The optimal density of sound-signals (information) is here the issue.

But we should not be led to think that the complexity of contemporary music is some sort of independent fact. This would be flatly false. A romantic symphony might, *in fact*, be much more complex than many modern works. The point is that in the former case 'complexity' is aesthetically irrelevant. In the latter case 'complexity' is tied to an aesthetic ideal. This means that it becomes essential to *understand* the music in quantitative terms. By the same token 'quantity' is seen as a qualitative term. (In the technological understanding of being 'quality' becomes a quantitative term; a quality is one, externally related 'parameter' that can correctly be predicated of some object.)

It is not possible to account for the meaning of 'complexity' without bringing in other concepts. When 'complexity' is an aesthetic ideal this means that tonal musical language cannot be used. This, latter, musical language is internally related to human gestures, dancing, emotive words and spoken language in general. One could say that it is about the human soul and, ultimately, about wondering at the world. 'Complexity' is of no aesthetical importance here. In order to create complex music the relationships between notes must be made *external*, that is; formal. Now the composer is free to choose the set of formal relationships he or she is going to deploy. The composer is also free to choose the sound-sources (they need not be conventional instruments). The 'sounding stuff' now used is a musical material. This means that the sounding stuff has, by itself, no meaning; it is not internally connected to human emotions, gestures, etc. (If it were, the composer would not be free to establish formal relationships at will.)

But is not the musical material used in contemporary music quite often to a substantial extent tonal and so in itself meaningful? The question one should ask here is this: Do we judge the worth of a work on the basis of how well it conforms to the aesthetical ideals of tonal music? If we do, why would we call the work a piece of contemporary music (instead of pastiche) in the first place? If we do not, then this shows that the 'tonal meaning' is only secondary. The composer is free to determine how audible this meaning is allowed to be and we have no grounds for blaming his judgement in this respect. This is because he only uses the tonal elements as a material.

When a composer works with musical *material* aiming at complexity it is of primary interest that he can give coherence to his material. The *structure* of the musical work is internally connected with its aesthetic value which is expressed in terms of complexity. (Structure should not be confused with form. The former is something we may *detect*, the latter is a part of *understanding*.) In order to manage the composer needs some tools for *controlling* his material. 'Control' is possible and necessary in connection with material. The tonal language cannot be controlled since here 'meaning' is pre-established through general standards of understanding. (To change this language in some respects is still to remain within it.) When this meaning is lacking it is necessary to use some means of control in order to create coherence. The more minute the control of a work is the more aesthetic value can be ascribed to it. This is of course connected with complexity; to control a simple process is of no interest. (Instances of non-control, for instance improvisation and chance, very clearly do not contradict the general importance of control.)

It might be objected that what I say is relevant only to serial music. I doubt that this is so, though it would take too much space to show it. I must confine myself to some hints only. Take for instance John Cage's idea that chance-music would be a rejection of calculation in music. I think he is thoroughly mistaken. The concept of chance is connected with an extreme form of calculative thinking. (This is what Hacking shows in his *The Taming of Chance*. See Hacking (1990).) 'Chance' would have been a completely useless concept to Mozart and this is because rigid musical calculation was foreign to him. Chance-operations are not 'connected' with calculation, they *are* a form of calculation. This becomes clear in the following statement by Tom Johnson (though he might not like to see himself quoted in this connection):

> A work like this ('Empty Words') represents a tremendous a-mount of labour, and I think that is an important point. By now, everyone knows that Cage constructs his works by chance operations, via the I Ching, but I think there is insufficient appreciation for the countless hours of tedious calculations which his method requires. In this case, for example, every single element, sometimes only a single letter, was carefully selected from the Thoreau text by means of random numbers from 1 to 64, and then written down in neat columns in stenographer's notebooks. Further chance operations were used to determine punctuation, spacing, and other formal elements. By the time one puts together a page or two of text by this method, many hundreds of chance operations are required. (Johnson 1989, 190)

Johnson not only describes the 'tedious calculations' but also thinks this calculation should be more *appreciated*. I think he is right; calculation is part of the aesthetic worth of the work.

What about minimal music? Many composers and listeners seem to think that in minimal music complexity and calculation have given place to simplicity and spontaneity. Only, the former often forget this idea when they speak about composing. LaMonte Young, one of the key-figures of minimal music, is interested in repetition (the principal technique of minimal music) because it 'demonstrates control' (Nyman 1974, 123). Indeed we find in minimal music all those concepts that are central to both serialism and the music of Cage; complexity, structure, control etc. When concepts are essential, express our ideals, then the description of one of the concepts will bring in others that are essential. Here we see how it works from the standpoint of 'material':

> [W]hen consonant harmonies are run through any kind of repetition process, [...] the emphasis on process means that the primary material may be quite insignificant [...]. (Nyman 1974, 144)

That is, 'material' cannot be described without reference to 'structure' and 'control' (conjoined in 'repetition process'). – Another example:

> The piece [Jon Gibson's *Melody*] has an absolute consistency about it, and it makes those very very smooth gradual transitions which can only be achieved when one employs a strict logical process of some sort. (Johnson 1989, 179)

Here we see how the very idea of minimalism (the 'very smooth gradual transitions') is dependent on control which, again, would be pointless if it were simply about simple things. But it is not. Or, as Ivan Moody puts it (commenting on Gorecki's *Miserere*):

> The simplicity of the material used in this work would make it extremely dangerous in the hands of a less gifted composer. What sets Gorecki apart is the consummate control which he exercises over every aspect of his musical material: the number of repetitions is always carefully controlled, the harmonic progressions tightly reined, the dynamics minutely shaded. (Moody 1992, 284)

What *appears* to be simple is actually *rigorously controlled* – it is *complex*. This is what gives the work its value. – It would be possible to find countless examples that show how a group of concepts (not a closed group) that are external to human responses, constitute the essence of contemporary music. This essence is about controlling and demanding by methods external to human responses and human understanding.

Final remarks

Economics is only one aspect of the technological understanding of being, though an important aspect undoubtedly. One might even say that not only the distinction between science and technology but also the distinction between economics and the two former ones has become less clear. Innovation, application and resources cannot be separated. It seems as if the meaning of these activities were united in the power of controlling things that they provide us with. This is a sort of demand in itself; the ability to control is an ability to extend the possible range of what can be demanded.

Naturally I do not make any quantitative claims about the prevalence of the technological understanding of being. Neither has my main point been to show that the technological understanding with its external relationships is philosophically flawed. Musically speaking this is a wholly irrelevant issue. But not only musically. The problem cannot be solved by way of philosophical argument since it is about our way of living and our way of understanding being; the problem is moral and it is such also in music. Our attitude of demanding and controlling is irreconcilable with wondering at being. I think that the state of contemporary music shows how deep this problem is; in music, and in art in general, there is no necessity – only freedom. This is so with one exception only: an artist must be truthful. This is no recommendation. Art *is* that which is true but the truth might not always be attractive. Contemporary music shows us what it means to be truthful today. (Kitsch is also true in a sense since it is an expression of the *longing* for beauty – not of beauty itself.)

It is often thought that music, and art in general, can present to us ideas other than those of everyday life with its business, politics and news. Certainly music can remind us of and make vivid to us more profound ideas *insofar as we subscribe to those ideas*. But music has no power to impose on us (or even authentically present to us) ideas that are no longer ours.

9 Law, ethics and the economy

Vivan Storlund

History offers an interesting pattern concerning the social effects of technological development and economic progress. Technological innovations, since
inventions in agriculture in the 11th - 13th centuries to the boost in technological innovations in the 1970s appear to generate similar effects – social
marginalisation.[1] Such historical facts stand in blatant contrast to the prevailing theoretical view, which since the times of Adam Smith and Jeremy
Bentham is based on the idea that economic activities, when freely pursued,
will work to the greatest happiness of the greatest number. This legacy is
very much alive today, at an economic and political level, while its social
consequences induce us to find an exit to these problems in notions about
social justice and ethics. Thus, what theories hold to be a cohesive force in
society appears, at some point, to become a disintegrating one, a development against which law appears toothless. A reassessment of the notion of
the rule of law is therefore necessary, if we are to make sense of social justice
and ethics in present day social arrangements.

What are our legal means of coming to grips with economic conduct, when
this creates unreasonable burdens on people? I will here show that because of
the way the rule of law is perceived, there are insufficient means of attaining
such conduct, although it is generally perceived as unjust. One explanation
to this is that the notion of the rule of law, or *Rechtsstaat*, as it now stands,
was constructed according to the world view of classical economics, primarily
designed to regulate business dealings among peers.[2]

---

[1]Excellent illustrations of this offer among others Huberman (1968), and most of Galbraith's (1987) production, such as *Economics in Perspective* (1987). For a scrutiny of
social marginalisation in the middle ages see Tuchman (1979, 365-97), Storlund (1990).

[2]See Storlund (1992a, sections II. 5 and 6) for a scrutiny of how the 19th century notion
of the rule of law crystallized. Its use in asymmetrical contractual relations, is illustrated

When we are concerned with business dealings, there are potentials for a legal assessment of economic conduct, because we are, in principle, concerned with commensurable transactions. It is when this legal model is extended outside its proper scope that the social effects of economic conduct became largely out of reach for an effective legal assessment. An assessment of conduct will most probably be made by a court of law but, in my view, this assessment enters too late to be constructive, and does often place an unreasonable burden of reaction and proof on the 'weaker' party.[3]

As soon as we move outside business dealings proper, or when our scope of inquiry is extended to third parties, we are dealing with relations which, as the legal tradition now stands, become unattainable, because we are dealing with 'incommensurable entities'. This englobes a number of situations, from business versus consumers and other asymmetrical transactions, to the effect of changes in the business world on household economies, of which there has been ample illustrations since the period of 'casino economy' in the 1980s.

The issue at stake here is the legitimizing force the legal tradition accords property, a legacy of John Locke.[4] As an effect of this, the only terrain a legal assessment will get proper access to is that of people, holding equal bargaining power, who are involved in mutual transactions.[5] Here we are in the terrain of classical economics. But even here, when the symmetry offered by equal bargaining power is lacking, the conditions are more often than not a fiction rather than a reality for a considerable part of economic life, where small and middle size enterprises have to compete with increasingly large corporations. In order to perceive the nature of the problem, we need to direct simultaneous attention to both law and economics, and to the steering effect the theories of economics and law, which crystallized in the 18th and 19th centuries, have on the legal administration of economic and social affairs in the late 20th century.

John Kenneth Galbraith has repeatedly pointed at the stronghold of economic theories, and their legitimizing force in the pursuit of economic interests, and how these are void of any sense of social or moral obligation:

Things may be less than good, less than fair, even less than tol-

---

in Storlund (1992b, Chap III and IV).

[3] I have illustrated this problem in the case of labour law and industrial relations in Storlund (1994).

[4] *"Political power* then I take to be *a Right* of making Laws with Penalties of Death, and consequently all less penalties, for the Regulation and Preserving of Property, and of employing the force of the community, in the Execution of such Laws, and in the defence of the Commonwealth from Foreign Injury, and all this only for the Public Good." (Locke 1965, 308).

[5] Illustrated in Storlund (1992b).

erable; that is not the business of the economist as an economist. Because of the claim of economics that it should be considered a science, it must separate itself from the justice or injustice, the pain and hardship of the system. The economist's task is to stand apart, analyze, describe and where possible reduce to mathematical formulae, but not to pass moral judgement or be otherwise involved.

In the administration of law, we find a corresponding delimitation of 'the possible', the anatomy of which Lars Hertzberg describes as follows:

> Some aspects of the legal order seem to be designated primarily to *uphold* certain prevalent practices or generally accepted norms of conduct. They do so by clearly delimiting the forms of conduct required, and by enforcing those requirements [...] the concerns expressed in the law will be held to determine, roughly, what may or may not count as a just application of the law in question; what sorts of considerations are to be held relevant in applying it; etc. In this way, those concerns can be said to delimit the autonomy of legal reasoning. (Hertzberg 1981, 102-103)

We are hostages of both a legal and economic logic, to which we need to find an exit. Here we should, as Hertzberg suggests, get clear about the logical character of legal reasoning. This implies that we get to understand the relations between legal and non-legal concepts and ways of reasoning (Hertzberg 1981, 102). Hertzberg assesses what is involved in legal decision-making. He points out that the general way of explaining legal decision-making as deductive reasoning is a misleading one. It does not say anything false, but it fails to explain anything. This does not just mean that it fails to represent the manner in which judges actually arrive at decisions, but, more important, he notes, "contrary to what it claims, this view cannot account for our ability to distinguish between correct and incorrect decisions" (Hertzberg 1981, 97). Hertzberg suggests that we turn things round, and says that

> for a representation of those principles to be correct, it must *reflect* the way in which we actually draw the distinction between valid and invalid arguments in particular cases [...] we do not reason like this in a particular case because we accept these principles, but rather these general principles are acceptable to us since this is how we reason in a particular case. (Hertzberg 1981, 97-98)

And here the steering effect of theories is crucial for how we perceive social reality and argue about cases in legal terms. What is involved is that lawyers and judges play the same 'game' and this makes an exit difficult (Hertzberg 1981, 101).

Today's agenda

Times of crisis place established truths to a test. Despite the recognition of a series of human rights and social welfare provisions, an increasing number of people are today economically and socially marginalized. This is an indication that the legal tradition has not been able to secure human rights and social welfare, as this was intended by public policy. In what way does law run short of making legal policy a reality for people, at least as it was intended until about the 1970s, when the economic recession associated with the oil crisis started a new trend in public policy?[6]

We are here faced with a situation where law in operation is increasingly at odds with peoples sense of justice. This indicates an expanding discrepancy between formal and informal perceptions of the 'legal order'. It is when this agreement is lacking, that we feel compelled to assess the legal tradition critically, because, as Roland Dworkin notes, law is our most structured and revealing social institution (Dworkin 1986, 11).

In order to come to grips with this discrepancy, we need to contrast our theoretical legacies with present day circumstances. On this point, the following observation made by Hertzberg is a worthwhile start:

> Judicial decisions, just like the judgements of lawyers, are based on reasons, and the reasons that both have been taught to consider relevant are of the same kind. (Hertzberg 1981, 101)

When the reason, which steers law becomes too much at variance with the general sentiment of fairness, the relevance of these reasons has to be reconsidered. What do they presuppose? To what extent do they give a fair representation of factual social arrangements and human affairs?

Changing social contexts

Behind the change in public policy in the 1970s we have a changing economic environment, which is not sufficiently reflected either in present day economic

---

[6]This trend and its implications for industrial relations and trade union rights have been treated in Storlund (1992b).

or legal analysis. A first step, therefore, in trying to make sense of the idea of the rule of law, we need to assess critically the theoretical premises of this notion, by directing attention to the context in which it was advanced and why, and identify its shortcomings in today's context. This I conceive of as a precondition in order to propose remedies to the notion of the rule of law, which will satisfy our sense of justice.

Leo Huberman has given a colourful account of the social context in which the economic theories emerged, which have exercised a strong steering effect both on the legal tradition and the way business is legitimised today.

> [T]he economists at the time of the Industrial Revolution developed a series of laws which, they said, were as true for the social and economic world as were the laws of the scientist for the physical world. They formulated a set of doctrines which were the "natural laws" of economics [...]. They wouldn't argue about whether the laws were good or bad. No point in such a discussion. Their laws were fixed, eternal. (Huberman 1968, 204)

These doctrines and concepts were developed to provide a breach against mercantilist regulation, restriction and restraint. Adam Smith was first, in 1776, at the beginning of the industrial revolution. His ideas were developed and expanded by his followers, such as Thomas Robert Malthus and David Ricardo, when the industrial revolution was making headway, adding "natural laws" of their own, which fitted the conditions of the times" as Huberman puts it (Huberman 1968, 206). Galbraith has also repeatedly noted how the classical economists were spokesmen of a new ruling class in a new economic order, speaking to and for their constituency (Galbraith 1987, 87).

At a legal level there was a corresponding activity. This was the 19th century codification activities, which constituted the theoretical transition from the old legal order to a new one. Enlightenment thinkers like Thomas Hobbes and Locke had paved the way for an atomistic view of society and its inhabitants. When this new world outlook was transformed into legal language, concepts of Roman law were drawn upon, often forging original Roman notions in order to fit the social context, within which human relations were now transformed from status to contract.[7] By way of illustration, the French *code civile* dealt in close to 800 articles with property, whereas only 7 articles were devoted to labour. Huberman notes: "The Code was made by the bourgeoisie for the bourgeoisie; it was made by the owners of

---

[7] An illustration of this process for the employment relationship is given in Storlund (1992b), sections III.1.1, 1.2.

property for the protection of property".[8] This legacy of Roman law implied, according to Galbraith, "the right not only of enjoyment and use but also of misuse and abuse. Intrusion of them by others or the state would henceforth carry the burden of justification."[9]

The 19th century world view was permeated by an economic outlook, and this was reflected in the legal traditions which crystallized during this century. Gone were the old-fashioned notions of status, which made one person subdued to another. Industrialists and their workers, merchants and their clients, landlords and tenets were all equal contracting partners, with equal rights and obligations. These relations pertained to the sphere of private law, whereas the public sector was set to protect those rights and liberties which went along with the new order, within which property constituted a cornerstone.[10] The enlightenment project was completed. The world was inhabited by social atoms, who could go about maximising their happiness, which through the blessings of the invisible hand should work to the greatest happiness of the greatest number.

This should evidently not be read as a historical anecdote, but rather be contrasted to the social effects of industrialisation, which democracy, a tradition of human rights and social welfare were aimed at remedying during this century. It should be a reminder of how we have failed to adapt our theoretical tools to social and political changes, corresponding to those, which the classical economists and the 19th century tradition of the rule of law achieved, as part of the transition from mercantilism to industrialisation. The present agenda requires thus an adaptation of these schemes in order to give substance to a democratic form of government, human rights and social welfare, none of which formed part of the 18th and 19th century agenda.

The hidden agenda

Because theory has not been adapted to the changing economic, political and social environment, we operate with a hidden agenda, which steers our perception of matters under scrutiny. David Hume has noted that we take a lot on trust – as we have done. This is as such a practical necessity, but when we reach dead ends, we need to turn attention to what we have taken on trust, and make that our object of scrutiny, rather than a premise. And here the premises have to be contrasted to matters as they appear to different

---

[8]Huberman (1968, 158).
[9]Galbraith (1987, 19).
[10]Different aspects of this development has been traced in Storlund (1989), Storlund (1992b) and Storlund (1992a).

actors in the real world. In the field of economics, above all Huberman and Galbraith have made perceptive analysis, for which conclusions should be drawn in the field of law.

Already in the 1960s Galbraith pointed at how the theories of economists had little to do with the system then in operation, and this observation has lost none of its relevance since then. In *The New Industrial State* Galbraith (1968) gives a comprehensive analysis of changes in the economic world, and the failure of economists to draw conclusions of these changes in the nature of economic activity and the location of factual power, both in economic activity and in a wider social context. One explanation Galbraith offers for this is that for a long time nobody engaged in formal economic inquiry would consider that economic activity was associated with power. Instead the legacy of the classical economic tradition was adhered to, which pictured the business enterprise as a small entity, with the classical picture of price and wage setting etc (Galbraith 1968, 58-59).

> The shift of power has been disguised because, as was once true of land, the position of capital is imagined to be immutable. That power should be elsewhere seems unnatural [...]. (Galbraith 1968, 69)

Power associated with property, and how it should be administered is a problem which runs throughout history. Aristotle gives the following lucid analysis of this:

> [T]here is no limit to the end which acquisition [of goods] has in view, because the end is wealth in that form, i.e. the possession of goods. The kind which is household-management, on the other hand, does have a limit, since it is the function of household-management to acquire goods. So, while it seems that there must be a limit to every form of wealth, in practice we find that the opposite occurs: all those engaged in acquiring goods go on increasing their coin without limit, because the two modes of acquisition of goods are so similar. For they overlap in that both are concerned with the same thing, property; but in their use of it they are dissimilar: in one case the end is. sheer increase, in the other something different. (Aristotle 1987, 84)

The above distinction, made by Aristotle, is wanting in our theoretical schemes. In my view, it is the social consequences of this which induces us to reconsider the notion of the rule of law. Then as now, it is a question of the

power resident in economic life, and the extent to which it can be pursued
at the cost of human needs and concerns, i.e. the household economy. To
what extent does theory and law place limits to the extent to which economic
interests can be pursued at the cost of human ones?

We are here concerned with deep structural features in our theoretical
tradition and their reflection in legislation, which should not be confused
with protective provisions in fields such as labour or consumer law. Such
protective provisions enter, in my view, too late, and place an unduly heavy
burden of justification on the party which is in need of protection.

The problems thus lay at a deep level, out of reach of positive legislation.
This is illustrated by the ease with which social welfare provisions are now
dismantled, a trend which the western world has witnessed since the oil crisis
of the 1970s. It reveals the impotence of positive laws to secure interests
formerly protected by laws and institutions. It equally reveals how small
business and the household-economy competes on very unequal terms with
an increasingly international economy. And this despite, or perhaps because
of, increasingly efficient means of production, which, ironically enough, have
lead to an affluence of products, rather than a shortage to be shared, in
the affluent parts of the world. But this is not something new, neither are
its consequences. Huberman gives a penetrating account of factual power
relationships in the 1930s. He points at how monopoly industry in the early
part of the 20th century had lead to an over-accumulation of capital, one
central ingredient of the great depression of the 1930s. This abundance of
capital he comments as follows:

> Now that sounds funny. How could there be too much money?
> Were there no ways to be found for the useful employment of
> capital? [...] Surely there were a hundred and one businesses [...]
> were money could be invested? There were. Rural areas needed
> better roads, workers needed decent houses, and small businesses
> were crying for expansion – yet economists spoke of "surplus"
> capital. And there was no doubt of it – [...] Why? Because
> capital does not ask, "What is needed? Not at all. What it does
> ask is, "How much can I get for my money?" (Huberman 1968,
> 260–261)

This pursuit of power and its pecuniary and physic rewards, Galbraith
notes, is then as now, the black hole of mainstream economics (Galbraith
1987, 115). And it was even seen as a calling, as Max Weber has pointed
at, living as he did in the period, when the theoretical traditions we now
question, crystallized. I will therefore cite him at length, in order to convey

the flavour of the then prevailing world view, which really has not changed much in those quarters, where power lies:

> Man is dominated by the making of money, by acquisition as the ultimate purpose of his life. Economic acquisition is no longer subordinated to man as the means for the satisfaction of his material needs. This reversal of what we should call the natural relationship, so irrational from a naive point of view, is evidently as definitely a leading principle of capitalism as it is foreign to all peoples not under capitalistic influence. At the same time it expresses a type of feeling which is closely connected with certain religious ideas. If we thus ask *why* should 'money be made out of men', Benjamin Franklin himself, although he was a colourless deist, answers in his autobiography with a quotation from the Bible, [...] 'Seest thou a man diligent in business? He shall stand before kings' (Proverbs 22:29). The earnings of money within the modern economic order is, so long as it is done legally, the result and the expression of virtue and proficiency in a calling [...].

> In truth this peculiar idea, so familiar to us today, is in reality so little a matter of course, of one's duty in a calling, is what is most characteristic of the social ethic of capitalistic culture, and is in a sense the fundamental basis of it. It is an obligation which the individual is supposed to feel and does feel towards the content of his professional activity, no matter in what it consists, in particular no matter whether it appears on the surface as a utilisation of his personal powers, or only of his material possessions (as capital). (Weber 1983, 114-115)

Then as now, a problem is that we take the "natural laws" of economics on trust, backed by legal theories and regulation. We have thus failed to develop theoretical tools, through which to allow a household point of view to compete on equal terms with that of the economy for its own sake, a distinction advocated by Aristotle. Instead we have a long series of theoretical legacies, which sustain business as it stands today. These have to be questioned, if we are to provide viable alternatives to today's legacies. This entails making power visible and linking responsibility to that power. In present day schemes these are largely lacking, as Galbraith frequently has pointed out. He remarks that in the big corporations which possess factual power on the market, the 'owners' of the corporation, the stockholder does not typically identify himself with the corporation:

normally his only concern is that it returns him as much money
as possible. If he can get more income or capital gain with equal
security elsewhere, he sells and invests there. No sense of loyalty
– no identification with the goals of the enterprise – normally
prevents him doing so. (Galbraith 1968, 160)

Law and ethics

In the same vein as economic theories still to a great extent picture economic
activity as that pursued by the small enterprise, which is submitted to the
free market forces, so law pictures human and social relations in equally
distorting terms.

Contract and authority were the simplistic concepts through which 19th
century societies were pictured, during an epoch which constituted one of
the most profound social changes in western history. True, we sometimes
need to simplify in order to perceive some basic structures in the complex
reality we are faced with, but to make this simplified scheme the point of
departure for the legal regulation of complicated social issues simply begs for
trouble. Behind this constellation of contract and public authority we have a
legacy of Hobbes and Locke, a mixture which I have nowhere seen so nakedly
expressed as by Locke in his characterization of political power.[11] This is a
legal legacy we live with today, which corresponds to the legacy of Smith and
his followers in economic terms.

In order to come to grips with ethical questions associated with the economy, economic and legal matters have to be considered in conjunction. In
this exercise attention has to be paid to the steering effect of the theoretical schemes which reside behind economic, legislative and administrative
practices, and their implications for social and human conditions.

A challenge we face today is thus to bring theoretical reflection in line
with the concerns and needs of living human beings out in societies, as we
have them today. If we contrast this need to that of a century back, we will
catch the present concern in a nutshell. One hundred years ago, a major
concern was to achieve general franchise, and to allow workers to combine in
order to defend their interests against a ruthlessly pursued industrialisation
process. Since the early part of this century we have had a democratic form of
government which allowed the whole population to partake in the running of
the social enterprise of government. Despite this 'best form of government',
government by the people, there has, during this century, been what seems to

---

[11]See above, footnote 4.

be an endless need to confirm an ever increasing number of (human) rights. This need of rights stems, in my view, from the inadequate reflection in theory, and as a derivation, in law of the social phenomena it was designed to regulate one century ago. It is this misrepresentation of social reality that is involved, when we express concerns about ethics in an economic context.

The theoretical and legal transition from status to contract left the contracting partners in the same asymmetrical constellation they had been in before, but short of the obligations the masters had concerning the wellbeing of their workers. (Whether they lived up to these obligations is another story). One reason why this aspect did not press itself too much on those who contributed to this scheme, is that formal equality and freedom of contract were the major focus of theoretical perception. This asymmetrical constellation between the contracting partners, and the heavy burden obligations associated with the contract meant for the weaker party, I see as a major explanation why we have been in such a need of basic and legal rights during this century. This brings to the fore law's role in this process. Law was the means through which to provide protection, when social welfare provisions were introduced, but a legal positivist approach contributed to keeping the misleading premises and thereby substantive aspects out of sight during long periods of this century.

We here need to go back to Hertzberg's observation about the reasons.[12] These pertain to the theoretical premises and the steering effect they have on the legal administration of justice, and how the autonomy of legal reasoning is thereby delimited.[13] Attention should, therefore, be directed towards how these conceptual schemes are at work today, in the context of a concentration and internationalisation of capital and an expanded administration, which reflects changes in the political, economic and social environment.

In her book *Ethics of an Artificial Person*, Elizabeth Wolgast (1992) has made a comprehensive inventory of the effects of Hobbes' legacy in present day theoretical and legal schemes. She scrutinizes how artificial persons or agents are embedded in our institutions and professions, and how they are defined and conceived. She investigates how such arrangements, with their rationale and paradigm, relate to morality, and points at a deep and intractable dissonance between Hobbes' agency paradigm and that of moral theory, which represents a paradigm of autonomous and responsible persons (Wolgast 1992, 2). She displays how and why institutional practices can have priority over moral claims, in a way that frustrates moral evaluation.

And law plays its part in blocking such evaluation. What is needed today

---

[12]See above, p. 144.
[13]See above, p. 143.

is therefore to devise an alternative departure, which will make presumptions
of formal equality the object of scrutiny rather than the point of departure.
This will allow an assessment of human behaviour with focus on autonomous
and responsible persons. In order to do this we should contrast theory with
the practical working of social institutions, as seen from a human perspective.

When general franchise and the organization into trade unions and other
interest groups allowed ordinary people, who had been very unequal contracting partners in the 19th century, to catch up with their stronger counterparts,
and social welfare was introduced, aimed at providing greater security, we
suddenly wake up to see that we are surrounded by untouchable 'artificial
persons'! From Hobbes we have the legacy of the state; political and public
power as untouchable, in the sense that power is enough to legitimize its use.
In the legal positivist orientation, sovereignty and power was taken on board
unquestioned, a legacy of Bentham and John Austin.[14] We therefore take
this power as a point of departure without much questioning. This legacy
has since the 19th century been qualified by the requirements that public
(administrative) power be exercised in a neutral and objective manner, con-
fined to laws and regulations only. This places the social security officer who
turns down a client, because her distressed situation does not happen to co-
incide with the scenarios which came to the law-drafters mind, on pair with
the ministerial officer who is engaged in plans and transactions involving big
business. Not much imagination is needed to see that rule-following is of
very different kinds in these two situations.

In economic life again, we still talk about employer and employee, which is
most peoples' link to business life, because it constitutes a work place. Since
the early part of the century, an employer of flesh and blood has increasingly
turned into an artificial person, who's business is operated through agents.
We learn from a handbook of agency that "[m]ost of the world's work is
performed by agents", and on this theme Wolgast gives us a thoroughgoing
analysis of agency in different walks of life, and the moral implications of
these schemes.[15] She notes that

> [t]his depersonalization extends even wider. In economics, the
> family appears as a unit with specific functions – with income,
> demographic features, and spending habits. And the nation is
> made up of such entities; all can be dealt with for social and
> economic purposes without using any language that would trig-
> ger moral inferences. Thus, thanks to this framework, economics

---

[14]See Raz (1980, 11) and Tolonen (n.d., 24).
[15]See Wolgast (1992, chapter 7).

and much social theory, albeit unwittingly, sanction the dehumanization of persons and the neglect of them as moral entities.

Wolgast stresses that work done in the instrumental positions of agency is fundamentally different, morally different from work done even partly through one's own initiative and decision, with both pervasive and inescapable moral hazards as a result (Wolgast 1992, 129-130).

And when a wrong or injustice is done, the arrangement of artificial persons easily leads to moral frustration and agentless deeds. The number of agents involved and their roles protect them and insures that 'Nobody does whatever is done'. Such arrangements, Wolgast notes,

> leads a chase through warrens and thickets of roles, instructions, interpretations and chains of command. With increasing distance between order and action, with the attendant increase in ambiguity, responsibility is harder to retrieve from the cracks. Thus, it seems that institutions themselves are the problem. (Wolgast 1992, 35)

A human perspective

If we approach our theoretical schemes, and their effects on social cooperation from the point of view of living persons, in contrast to contractual relationships, agents and public authority, we will perceive the multiple roles people assume, with equally multiple effects. This will require attention to be directed towards social and human intercourse instead of the theoretical notions of contract and public authority.

In the prevailing (positivist) legal tradition this presents a challenging task, and what will proceed will only be tentative and fragmentary, but still an attempt at catching problems which raise concern about ethics today, which in my interpretation relate to the stronghold of economic and legal theories, and their shortcomings as indicated above.

How to come to grips?

The reason why we need to talk about ethics *and* the economy, is that because of the way business is now pursued and supported through public policy, an increasing number of people stand the risk of social marginalisation. Notwithstanding the bright prospects of an enhanced situation for the majority of people, which general franchise and the building of the welfare state could have made possible, the economic rationale underlying the legal tradition has contributed to the position where we stand today. As this situation is increasingly conceived of as unfair, and arouses moral resentment, we need to dig out the real human beings from behind the depersonalised notions of contractual partners and instrumental agents, whether they are agents of the state or agents in business life.

In order to give the human being primary concern we have to start from human beings in a real world context, and their interdependencies. Here Aristotle offers guidance. To him the state is an association intended to enable its members, in their households and the kinships, to live well; its purpose is a perfect and self-sufficient life.[16]

The good life, which Aristotle has designated as the ultimate purpose of government, requires a certain minimum supply of necessities. Property is one such necessary prerequisite to satisfy basic needs.[17] Property is thus a means for the end of satisfying basic needs, and thereby there is also a natural limit to the acquisition of property. But, as noted above, he points out that there is another kind of property-getting, to which the term 'acquisition of goods' applies, and it is due to this, he explains, that there is thought to be no limit to wealth or property.[18]

In a reassessment of our theoretical schemes formal equality has to give way for considerations of human capacities, inclinations and restraints. From this point we have to work ourselves forth to consider the interdependencies which exist in society. This will make our perspective relational and display the nature of human action. It will allow a moral evaluation of actions in all walks of life; how public power is administered, what effects economic transactions made by big corporations have on ordinary people's lives, etc. This requires a scheme which is sensitive to the human condition and human behaviour. Instead of a presumption of autonomous persons, which was part of the enlightenment scheme, we thus have to direct primary attention to human behaviour and institutions which infringe on the personal autonomy of other people. In contrast to the prevailing scheme which makes contractual obligations a heavy burden on an unequal contractual partner, focus has in this alternative scheme to be directed towards those who are in command of power over other people's conditions of life, and accord responsibility which stands in relation to that factual power.

This focus will allow us to see where true power lies and how it is used. It also allows us to perceive the genuine range of options different agents

---

[16]See Aristotle (1987, 196-198).
[17]See Aristotle (1987, 64-65).
[18]See Aristotle (1987, 81).

have as a matter of fact and how these are enhanced or restrained by laws and institutions. In this perspective much of our habitual ways of thinking must be reconsidered. We have to be attentive to social change and adjust the working of our institutions in ways which will preserve human and democratic values.

The deregulation of capital and exchange rates, a general feature of the 1980s, is part and parcel of the internationalization of capital. In this process national politicians have ceded much of the factual power they earlier possessed, which constitutes a decisive change, to which attention has to be directed. Instead of a focus on a redistribution of income among the population, governmental measures are now frequently directed towards defending the national economy against the effects of the 'free market forces'. These 'forces', which equals the movers of big capital thus hold a power which exceeds that of national politicians. As matters now stand, they are untouchable because of the way the frame within which they operate is legally constructed. They are artificial persons, or their actions are concealed from view because of the way economics and law are perceived and administered.

Paradigmatic shift

The theoretical scheme I propose draws inspiration from theories of (social) justice.[19] These theories constitute a decisive break with the traditions I have critically assessed above. One important aspect of theories of justice is that they propose an assessment of existing institutions. This constitutes a decisive alternative to the value neutrality required by classical theories and a scientific approach to economics and law. And, what is vital, theories of justice direct attention to human beings and their particular situation, to which the classical theories are insensitive.

If ideas of justice are to be taken seriously, in the sense that law be sensitive to human beings, the most decisive change is required in our thinking, to be reflected in our theoretical schemes. Because if justice is taken seriously, whatever the institutional or social setting, peoples' personal autonomy should be respected, and if competing, accommodated. Thus if power is accompanied by responsibility, there will be a natural limit to how economic and political affairs can be pursued. This shall not be conceived of as an utopian notion, but as a tool, through which to assess if power is duly managed in a particular context. This is no easy point of departure, but it will

---

[19] I have in different respects drawn inspiration from John Rawls, David Miller, Wojciech Sadurski.

allow attention to be directed to the complexities of social life before a right has to be defended in a court of law.

10 Real freedom, democratic community and sustainable development as fundamental values in economic enquiry

Jan Otto Andersson

Introduction

Economic analysis is profoundly affected by values and ideologies. The utilitarian approach has imbued standard economics to such an extent that it has become difficult to distinguish "normative" or "welfare" economics from utilitarianism. But even in economics, there is a persevering consciousness of the problems inherent in utilitarianism and ethical hedonism.[1]

If the utilitarian approach, and the economic welfare theory related to it, is abandoned, we have to introduce other explicit values. If convention-

---

[1] The seventh point of the theoretical perspectives included in the constitution of the European Association for Evolutionary Political Economy (EAEPE) expresses the need for an alternative to the utilitarian dominance in economic thinking:

> The enquiry is value-driven and policy oriented and recognizes the centrality of participatory democratic processes to the identification and evaluation of real needs – instead of a utilitarian outlook which separates considerations of means from those of ends, and judgements of facts from those of value, and which ignores social relations, conflicts and inequalities between the agents.

EAEPE was founded in 1989 to promote evolutionary and realistic approaches to economic theory and policy. Its soul of fire has been Geoff Hodgson, and its membership has increased to more than 600 in June 1994. I have taken part in its activities since its foundation.

ally conceived "utility", "welfare" or "happiness" are discarded, we need to replace them by other value- concepts, if we are to guide economic enquiry towards ethically acceptable and politically relevant theories. In this article I propose three value-concepts: "real freedom for all", "democratic communities" and "sustainable development", which I think should be used in combination as fundamental values for a reorientation of economics.

"Real freedom" is a value formulated on the level of the individual. "Democratic community" is a value pertaining to a collective of people. "Sustainable development" relates to the global and ecological system as a whole. It is hardly possible to derive one of these values directly from the other two. There are genuine conflicts between them. "Real freedom for all" may clash with either "democratic community" or "sustainable development", or it may make the other two values to conflict with each other. This means that we are often unable to say which ethical position or political solution is preferable in any absolute sense; we have to accept valuational differences and ethical compromises. It is, however, important to see the reasons for the conflicts and compromises as clearly as possible.

I first present and discuss the three fundamental values. I then proceed to discuss their relations to different schools of thought in economics.

Real freedom for all

In his book *Inequality Reexamined* Amartya Sen stresses the shift in attention from achievements (such as utility or living standards) to resources (such as primary goods). This also represents a shift in attention towards freedom:

> The strategy of judging individual advantage by the person's command over resources, as opposed to what the individual actually achieves, is to refocus our vision from achievement to the means of freedom, and that is, in an obvious sense, a homage to freedom. (Sen 1992, 37)

However, Sen wants to take one step further towards focusing on freedom itself, rather than on the means to freedom, by shifting attention from the command over resources to what a person, in fact, can do or be.

> The resources a person has, or the primary goods that someone holds, may be very imperfect indicators of the freedom that the person really enjoys to do this or to be that. (ibid. 37-38)

Sen's proposed solution is to introduce the concept "capability", which he defines as a combination of functionings (beings and doings) that a person can achieve. It reflects a person's freedom to lead one type of life or another (ibid. 40). The capability approach puts emphasis both on the intrinsic value of individual freedom in a free society and on the instrumental value of the freedom to achieve well-being. Sen underscores the difference between the capability approach and other approaches to individual and social evaluations, such as the Rawlsian system based on primary goods, Dworkin's analysis based on resources, or the traditional real income-approaches. However, it builds on the same general evaluative foundation, since all these approaches are concerned with the extension of the freedom of the individuals to choose what kind of life they live.

What makes Sen's approach so appealing is that it focuses so clearly on *real* or *substantive* freedom, not only on formal freedom or on the distribution of the means for freedom. What also makes it appealing is the effort to relate the demands of equality to the demands for freedom. The equality of freedom to pursue our ends – i.e. the equality of capabilities to function – should be the basic equality looked for in a just society.

This attempt to connect freedom and equality is reminiscent of that of Marx. In an often quoted passage from the first book of *Capital* he expresses the ruling principle of communism as "the full and free development of every individual":

> Fanatically bent on making value expand itself, he [the capitalist] ruthlessly forces the human race to produce for production's sake; he thus forces the development of the productive powers of society, and creates those material conditions, which alone can form the real basis of a higher form of society, a society in which the full and free development of every individual forms the ruling principle. (Marx 1920, 603)

Robert van der Veen interprets "full and free development of every individual" to mean maximizing the *real freedom* of the worst-off group in analogy with the Rawlsian difference principle, but applied to real freedom instead of to income or primary goods (van der Veen 1991, 32-35). I find this interpretation to be very similar to the capability approach; distributive justice means to maximize the capability to function or the real freedom to achieve of the least advantaged group.

There are some interesting differences between the approaches of van der Veen and Sen: van der Veen wants to compensate for an individual's lack of earning capacity, whereas Sen also considers the capacity to transform incomes into achievements; Veen sticks strictly to the difference principle, whereas Sen is prepared to take into account the losses of real freedom required to raise the capabilities of the worst-off – but basically their ethical standpoints are the same.

Real freedom involves the capacity to recognize adequately one's own important purposes, and to overcome one's emotional fetters, as well as being free of external obstacles. As Taylor emphasizes, this requires a certain degree of self-understanding. Freedom cannot be understood just as an opportunity concept. (Taylor 1985, 228-229) This implies a radical break with orthodox economics, and makes the crucial distinction between real human needs and subjective volatile desires.

The first fundamental value to guide economic enquiry should therefore be "real freedom for all" or "the greatest capability to achieve for everyone". When constructing a welfare theory for the aggregate of individuals we should elaborate our main concepts, such as efficiency, equality and welfare, in terms of real freedom, rather than utility, consumption or income.

Democratic communities

To focus on the freedom and the capability to function of the individuals may involve a downgrading of the value of the community. Can the collective be seen as purely instrumental for the full and free development of its individual members? According to the doctrines of social contract theory and to certain forms of utilitarianism society is constituted by individuals for the fulfillment of ends which are primarily individual. Such a position can be called "political atomism" (Taylor 1985, 187). It is deeply ingrained in economic thinking since *homo oeconomicus* is very similar to the individual presupposed by political atomism. He is far from the social animal formulated by Aristotle.[2]

If we agree that social processes are crucial for the formation of the tastes, desires and beliefs of human beings, then we cannot take these as given and

---

[2]The fourth point in EAEPE:s theoretical perspectives underlines the difference between an atomistic and a social conception of the human beings:

> The concern is to address and encompass the interactive, social process through which tastes are formed and changed, the forces which promote technological transformation, and the interaction of these elements within the economic system as a whole – instead of a theoretical framework that takes individuals and their tastes as given, technology as likewise exogenous, and with production separated from exchange.

derive the institutions for a good society from them. We cannot e.g. treat the market as an ideal order without considering the effects of a market society on the whole of society and its members. Even if we put the free individual at the center stage we cannot ignore the necessary social conditions for the development of free individuals.

Taylor makes this point cogently:

> The crucial point here is this: since the free individual can only maintain his identity within a society/culture of a certain kind, he has to be concerned about the shape of this society/culture as a whole [...]. It is important to him that certain activities and institutions flourish in society. It is even of importance to him what the moral tone of the whole society is – shocking as it may be to libertarians to raise this issue – because freedom and individual diversity can only flourish in a society where there is a general recognition of their worth. (Taylor 1985, 207)

A most forceful critique of *homo oeconomicus* is presented in "For the Common Good" by the economist Herman E Daly and the philosopher John B Cobb.

> Economics based on *Homo economicus* as self-interested individual commends policies that inevitably disrupt existing social relationships [...]. We believe human beings are fundamentally social and that economics should be refounded on the recognition of this reality. We call for rethinking economics on the basis of a new concept of *Homo economicus* as person-in-community. (Daly and Cobb 1989, 164)

Daly and Cobb discuss the concept of community in depth and put forward a definition with strong normative elements. According to them a society should not be called a community unless it fulfills four criteria:

1. Membership in the society should contribute to self-identification. 2. The members participate extensively in the decisions by which their lives are governed. 3. The society as a whole takes responsibility for the members. 4. The society shows respect for the diverse individuality of its members. (ibid. 172)

This "community", however, is an ideal rather than a description of societies in general. The concept "person-in-community" then becomes an abstraction which is difficult to use in descriptive analysis. "Person-in-society" would probably be a better starting point for economic enquiries. However, the "community" of Daly and Cobb is a desirable society, which could be renamed "democratic community" and used as a valuational foundation.

A democratic community is desirable both instrumentally – being important for the realization of real freedom for everybody – and intrinsically. Its intrinsic value can be seen when there is a conflict between individual real freedom and democratic community. E.g. if uncontrolled migration threatens to disrupt a society, it should have the right to restrict the free movement of people, or, if too many in a society choose a life-style that is not affordable and therefore undermines the functioning of the community, it should be possible to impose certain obligations restricting the freedom of the individuals.

John Rawls has made an admirable effort to set forth the principles for a just and democratic society, based on a constitutional regime derived from a principle close to our "real freedom for all". By a "community" he means a society governed by a shared comprehensive religious, philosophical, or moral doctrine. He does not, however, consider such an ideologically narrow community to be a well-ordered democratic society, since it is guided by one ideology rather than by public reason and a political conception of justice (Rawls 1993, 42). One can, however, question whether not Rawls's requirements for a just democratic society constitute a moral doctrine in its own right. All persons are supposed to be ideal citizens, who are prepared to recognize each other as equals, and to accept the same conception of justice. Therefore, the "well-ordered democratic society", outlined by Rawls, can be reconciled with the value of "democratic community".

Although Rawls derives his conception of a democratic society from the principles of individual full autonomy and justice as fairness – i.e. from principles close to "real freedom for all" – he also acknowledges an intrinsic value, to it:

> A well-ordered political society is also a good in a second way. For whenever there is a shared final end, an end that requires the cooperation of many to achieve, the good realized is social: it is realized through citizens' joint activity in mutual dependence on the appropriate actions being taken by others. Thus, establishing and successfully conducting reasonably just [...] democratic institutions over a long period of time [...] is a great social good and appreciated as such. This is shown by the fact that a people refer to it as one of the significant achievements of their history. (ibid. 204)

Each conception of a collective implies the constitution of an "us" in relation to others. It requires criteria for membership and also some conception of the territory or property that belongs to the community. A community can make demands on its members that it cannot make on foreigners; but foreigners then do not have an equal right to be cared for by the community.

The most important identity-forming forces in history have been classes, religions and nations. Today – despite the internationalization of the economies – the nation states are still supposed to be that community through which people primarily identify themselves and through which they are able to make common decisions. The hollowing out of the nation states therefore implies a weakening of the possibilities to realize democratic communities. Therefore, efforts to restrengthen the capacity of the nation states to govern, or to create other collectives to democratically regulate the market forces should be important tasks for economic studies.

As argued by the social philosopher Michael Walzer a most urgent task is to extend democratic principles to the economic sphere. Large enterprises and workplaces, which affect the lives of several persons, should not be governed by individual owners. Democrats cannot accept that whole towns are owned and run by private owners, since this violates against the principles of democracy and equality as citizens, and the same principle should apply to large enterprises as well (Walzer 1993, 348-362).

The economists Samuel Bowles and Herbert Gintis have shown the importance of explicitly bringing in democratic values into economic enquiries. They find that the capitalist economy

> [...] not only fosters the exercise of unaccountable power, it also thwarts those forms of political learning-through-choosing by means of which democratic societies may come to deepen their fundamental political commitments and capacities. (Bowles and Gintis 1986, 90)

There are many other important contributions towards constructing the economy in accordance with democratic ideals, such as James Meade's "partnership economy" – *Agathotopia* – where different forms of ownership are mixed in such a way as to guarantee economic security for everyone (through a social dividend) and to strengthen worker participation in the running of the enterprises (through a system of worker share certificates).

Another effort, worthy of appreciation, is the radical democracy model elaborated by the neo-Marxian Budapest School. It tries to give formal democracy a new content by extending it to include equal rights of participation in all social decision-making processes. It implies the positive abolition of private property, self-management and the equal recognition (although not satisfaction) of all needs (Brown 1988, 134-146). The model requires the acceptance of some fundamental ethical principles: freedom, justice and an end to suffering. The spirit is captured by the concept of 'planetarian responsibility', which means that people behave responsibly by considering the effects of their actions on others (ibid. 147-148).

A commitment to the fundamental value of democratic communities would have profound consequences for economic analysis. Democracy could not be treated simply as a cost, which has become fashionable among economists eager to transfer power to agencies less dependent on popular support. An innocent example is to be found in one of the very first close-ups – "Opportunity Costs of Meetings" – in a fresh and widely acclaimed textbook. It has been estimated that business executives spend 288 hours a year in unnecessary meetings, and the pungent economist steps in improving the incentives to let everyone return to more productive tasks (Stiglitz 1993, 43).

Stiglitz cares a lot about decision making – whether it should be centralized or decentralized, how it should be structured, how to account for uncertainty, and so on – and although the book contains a short appendage of an appendix, called "Economic Organization and Political Freedom", there is nowhere in the text a reference to democracy or democratic decision-making . The list of the reasons for the failure of Soviet-style socialism does not mention the problems arising from lack of democracy (ibid. 1094-1097). The closest Stiglitz gets to problems related to democratic communities is the last student problem in the chapter on alternative economic systems:

> Imagine that you are sixty years old and you work for a worker cooperative in Yugoslavia. If you consider only your own self-interest, are you likely to support hiring more workers? Would you support long-term investments in capital? (ibid. 1109)

If economists were to consider alternatives, not only in terms of maximum net income or even real freedom, but also in terms of how well they correspond to and promote the ideal of democratic community – within the household, the firm or any other economic unit – their way of thinking would become less arrogant and misanthropic.

Sustainable development

In addition to real freedom for all and democratic communities we need a third concept to complete the set of fundamental values. The concept of sustainable development brings in an ecological and global dimension not fully covered by the other two values. The concepts of "all" and "community" might be streched to include ecological and global considerations, but we usually think of existing individuals and of our societies, and tend to forget the importance of finding the appropriate scale and pattern of human economic activities from the point of view of global sustainability.[3]

The term sustainable development has been interpreted in somewhat different ways, and a struggle over its meaning is probably going to be as intensive as the struggle over the meaning of "freedom" and "democracy". According to David Pearce

> sustainable *development* implies that the object of concern is the
> whole process of economic progress in which economies contribute
> to improvements in human welfare, however defined. [...] How
> sustainability comes about is the subject matter of most of the
> debate, but one theme is constant to all the discussions: sustain-
> ability means sustaining and augmenting natural environmental
> systems [...]. *Sustainability requires at least a constant stock of
> natural capital, construed as the set of all environmental assets.*"
> (Pearce 1992, 69)

Michael Jacobs finds a core meaning consisting of three elements. The first is the entrenchment of environmental considerations on all levels of economic policy-making. Sustainable development insists on the integration of the environment and the economy in both theory and practice (Jacobs 1991, 60). This requires a reconception of such central concepts as capital, income and welfare (Ekins 1992). Daly and Cobb shows how the concept of sustainability must influence the choice of discount rate in economic calculations. The discount rate must reflect only sustainable alternative uses of capital. "The allocation rule for attaining a goal efficiently (maximize present value) cannot be allowed to subvert the very goal of sustainable development that it is supposed to be serving!" (Daly and Cobb 1989, 75). They also point to the importance of choosing the right level of community when seeking to implement a sustainable development. To what extent should one country be allowed to draw on the ecological carrying capacity of another country and thus be unsustainable in isolation?

---

[3]The sixth point of EAEPE:s theoretical perspectives is a direct call for economics to take the natural environment more seriously:

> It is recognized that the socio-economic system depends upon, and is em-
> bedded in, an often fragile natural environment and a complex ecological
> system – instead of a widespread tendency to ignore ecological and environ-
> mental considerations or consequences in the development of theories and
> policy recommendations.

Second, sustainable development incorporates a commitment to equity, to a fair distribution between North and South as well as between our and future generations. This commitment is highly demanding, since mankind already has appropriated some 40 per cent of the terrestrial food supply, measured as the net primary productivity of solar energy reaching earth. At some point, the likely result is a chain reaction of environmental decline (Postel 1994, 7). Pearce finds that a sustainable economy should contribute to three types of justice: – justice to people within a generation, – justice to people between generations, and – justice to non-human sentient beings (Pearce 1992, 71-72).

The third element of the core meaning of sustainable development arises from the word "development". It is a wider concept than "growth" and includes the quality of the environment itself:

> [...] it is evident that national income does not record pollution levels or the beauty of natural scenery, both of which affect our welfare. They might also include factors such as the state of people's health and their level of education, the quality of work, the existence of cohesive communities, the vibrancy of cultural life. (Jacobs 1991, 61)

Jacobs thus comes close to subsuming "real freedom for all" and "democratic communities" under the concept of sustainable development. However, one can construct acceptable interpretations of sustainability, which could suppress both individual freedom and democratic communities in the sense given above. Therefore, rather than including real freedom for all and democratic communities in the concept of sustainable development, they should be kept as separate fundamental values. Sustainable development stresses the dimensions of global and intergenerational equity, as well as ecological balance, in a way freedom and democracy do not.

Sustainable development is not an absolute value, which has to be fulfilled before the other two can be considered. There can be more or less sustainability, greater or smaller risks for ecological catastrophes, as well as there can be different degrees of real freedom or vitality of democratic communities.

There are several important contributions trying to integrate ecological sustainability into economic analysis. With Geoffrey Hodgson I believe, that this is possible only through a radical rethinking of economic concepts and theories. He has made an admirable effort to "bring life back into economics", and suggests a reorientation that is not only methodological, but also takes into account the needs of the biotic system:

The history of mechanistic and equilibrium modeling in economics has sustained a view that the economic system may reach 'optima' which ignore the coupling of economic and biotic systems and have little or no regard to the limited natural resources on this planet. (Hodgson 1993, 267)

The value basis of different schools of economic thought

Which are the implications for an economic analysis that wants to take all three fundamental values into consideration? How do alternative economic schools stand up to this challenge? To answer these questions would need an extended program of research. Here I shall briefly reflect on how different schools seem to stand up to the challenge of integrating the fundamental values real freedom for all, democratic communities and sustainable development.

In a book edited by Douglas Mair and Anne G. Miller seven schools of thought in economics are described and compared. For each school the fundamental values related to it are listed. Mair and Miller express the results in the summary of each approach as follows:

The Austrian School
– Libertarian. Not known for their concern for others' welfare.
– Opponents of comprehensive economic planning.
– Suspicion of government's motives and capabilities (Mair and Miller 1991, 68).

The Neoclassical School (claims to be value-free)
– The satisfaction of wants is a good thing.
– A rational individual is best judge of own welfare; consumer sovereignty
– Individuals' optima are necessary for social optimum.
– Utilitarian maximization of 'sum total' of happiness
– given status quo; leads to a gradualist approach to reform.
– Pareto efficiency, given the status quo, takes priority.
– Libertarian. Anti-government intervention in markets. (ibid. 105)

The Chicago School
– Individual is best judge of own welfare.
– Consumer sovereignty.
– Libertarian.
– Anti-government intervention in markets. (ibid. 142)

The Orthodox Keynesian School
– Individual is best judge of own welfare; consumer sovereignty.
– Liberal.

– Role of government to influence aggregate demand to achieve full employ-
ment equilibrium. (ibid. 174)
The Post-Keynesian School
– Economists' values should be made explicit.
– Left of center mainly, concerned with unemployment, distribution of income
and power, and economic instability.
– Strong role for the state in a mixed economy, e.g. to curb power of large
business and of financial sector. (ibid. 203)
The Institutionalist (Evolutionary) School
– Non-materialistic values.
– Normative priorities; the direct implementation of the collective values of
a particular culture.
– Control of the economic system and its historical evolution. (ibid. 231)
Radical and Marxian Schools
– To create a decent and just society of fulfilled human beings. (ibid. 257)
– Expose the disadvantages of the capitalist system: conflictual non-harmo-
nious operation, discrimination, inequality and injustices, alienation, ineffi-
ciencies, instabilities. (ibid. 259)

This list gives a short, but general overview of the value positions of
the most influential schools of contemporary economic thought. It can be
criticized in different ways, but I do not think that it is grossly misleading.
Running down the list takes us from the most individualistic and right-wing
positions to the most collective and left-wing positions.

No-one of the schools seems to stress ecological sustainability directly.
The institutionalist concern for non-materialistic values can possibly be interpreted as a defence for the natural and cultural environment against a
rapacious productivism and consumerism. The list of disadvantages of the
capitalist system to be exposed by the radical economists does not directly
refer to the destruction of the natural environment, but it fits with some of
the aspects of sustainable development.

The first four schools do not emphasize democratic communities. Even
though the other three do not explicitly mention democratic communities,
they seem to be more aware of the importance of democratic and collective
means of influencing the economy. However, the recognition of a strong role
for the state or the wish to implement a just society are not necessarily
congruous with an emphasis on democratic communities.

Especially the three first schools stress individual freedom as a fundamental value, but it is doubtful whether they also would accept the value of "real
freedom for all" in the sense outlined above. The description of the central
value of radical and Marxian economics seems to come closest to this ideal.

It looks as if the post-Keynesian, the institutionalist and the radical and

Marxian approaches do have the best qualifications as constituents of a New Economics directed towards the simultaneous advancement of the three fundamental values. This fits the eighth point in EAEPE:s theoretical perspectives which acclaims the relevance of a list of named writers, the bulk of which are either institutionalists (John Commons, William Kapp, Gunnar Myrdal, Francois Perroux, Karl Polanyi and Thorstein Veblen) or post-Keynesians (Nicholas Kaldor, Joan Robinson and George Shackle). The list includes at least two "radical and Marxian economists" (Karl Marx and Michael Kalecki; Polanyi and Robinson are sometimes referred to as radical or neo-Marxian). The four remaining – John Maynard Keynes, Alfred Marshall, Adam Smith and Max Weber – are less easily classified, but I suspect that Marshall and Smith are included since much of their writings represent an evolutionary, rather than a typically neoclassical way of thinking. Max Weber belonged to the younger generation of the German Historical School, and can therefore be linked to the Institutionalist or Evolutionary School.

Mair and Miller do not treat a tradition which has been called "Humanistic Economics" (Lux and Lutz 1988), "Ecological Economics" (Martinez-Alier 1987) and "Living Economics" (Ekins 1986); (Ekins and Max-Neef 1992). This tradition, which includes Simonde de Sismondi, John Ruskin, John A Hobson and Richard Tawney, has been reinvigorated by "human scale" -economists, primarily Fritz Schumacher, "steady state" -economists, such as Herman E Daly, and Gandhian economists, e.g. Nandini Joshi. It explicitly introduces ecological and moral, even religious, considerations into economic enquiries, and it abhors acquisitive behaviour. The normative guideline of humanistic economics is said to be "material sufficiency and human dignity for all" (Lutz 1992, 110). This tradition thus emerges as the one most congruent with the three fundamental values elaborated above.

As a research tradition humanistic economics is, however, less developed then the seven schools compared by Mair and Miller. This is conceded by Ekins and Max-Neef, who want to combine different traditions into a New Economics:

> [...] living economics seeks to bring within a single frame of reference, in a mutually compatible way, some of the more significant streams of thought [...]: the evolutionary approach of Hodgson and Norgaard's coevolution; Etzioni's socio-economics; Lutz's humanistic economics; the ecological economics of Hueting and Pearce; and new approaches in development economics. This frame of reference provides a rich context for economic analysis in comparison with any of these streams in isolation, or compared to mainstream economics as a whole. (Ekins and Max-Neef 1992,

118-119)

The list should be broadened to include post-Keynesian, institutionalist and neo-Marxian approaches. It should also encompass writers, such as James Meade and Amartya Sen, who have received a high respect among orthodox economists, but who have been advancing theories and policies, which are consistent with the fundamental values proposed in this chapter.

Bibliography

Acton, H. (1971). *The Morals of Markets: An Ethical Exploration*, Longman Group Limited, London.

Adler-Karlsson, G. (1977). *Lärobok för 80-talet*, Prisma, Stockholm.

Adler-Karlsson, G. (1990). *Lärobok för 90-talet*, Prisma, Stockholm.

Aristotle (1987). *The Politics*, Penguin Classics, Harmondsworht.

Arrow, K. J. and Hahn, F. H. (1971). *General Competitive Analysis*, Holden Day, San Francisco.

Atkinson, A. B. (1992). Measuring poverty and differences in family composition, *Economica* 59: 1–16.

Atkinson, A. B. and Bourguignon, F. (1987). Income distribution and differences in needs, *in* G. Feiwel (ed.), *Arrow and the Foundations of the Theory of Economic Policy*, MacMillan, London.

Baker, J. (1992). An egalitarian case for basic income, *in* P. van Parijs (ed.), *Arguing for Basic Income*, Verso, London.

Barr, N. (1992). Economic theory and the welfare state: A survey and interpretation, *Journal of Economic Literature* 30: 741–803.

Bellah, R. and Madsen, R. (1992). *The Good Society*, Alfred A. Knopf, New York.

Bowles, S. and Gintis, H. (1986). *Democracy and Capitalism. Property, Community and the Contradictions of Modern Social Thought*, Basic Books, New York.

Brandt, R. (1979). *A Theory of the Good and the Bad*, Clarendon Press, Oxford.

Brandt, R. (1990). The science of man and wide reflective equilibrium, *Ethics* 100: 259–278.

Brown, D. M. (1988). *Towards a Radical Democracy. The Political Economy of the Budapest School*, Unwin Hyman, London.

Copleston, F. (1985). *A History of Philosophy*, Doubleday, New York.

Dalton, H. (1920). The measurement of the inequality of incomes, *Economic Journal* 30: 348–361.

Daly, H. E. and Cobb, Jr, J. B. (1989). *For the Common Good. Redirecting the Economy Toward Community, the Environment, and a Sustainable Future*, Beacon Press, Boston.

Daniels, N. (1979). Wide reflective equilibrium and theory acceptance in ethics, *Journal of Philosophy* 76: 256–282.

Debreu, G. (1959). *Theory of Value: An axiomatic analysis of economic equilibrium*, number 17 in *Cowles Foundation for Research in Economics at Yale University*, John Wilfrey & Sons, Inc., New York.

Diamond, C. (1991). Secondary sense, *in* C. Diamond (ed.), *The Realistic Spirit*, MIT Press, Cambridge, Mass., and London.

Dilman, I. and Phillips, D. (1971). *Sense and Delusion*, Routledge & Kegan Paul, London.

Douglas, M. (1986). *How Institutions Think*, Syracuse University Press., Syracuse, N.Y.

Durkheim, E. (1984). *The Division of Labour in Society*, Macmillan., London.

Dworkin, R. (1983). To each his own, *New York Review of Books* pp. 4–6.

Dworkin, R. (1986). *Law's Empire*, Fontana Press, London.

Ekins, P. (1986). *The Living Economy. A New Economics in the Making*, Routledge & Kegan Paul, London.

Ekins, P. (1992). A four-capital model of wealth creation, *in* P. Ekins and M. Max-Neef (eds), *Real-Life Economics. Understanding Wealth Creation*, Routledge, London.

Bibliography

Ekins, P. and Max-Neef, M. (1992). *Real-Life Economics. Understanding Wealth Creation*, Routledge, London.

Ellul, J. (1965). *The Technological Society*, Jonathan Cape, London. Translated by J.Wilkinson.

Elster, J. (1985). *Explaining Technical Change*, Cambridge University Press and Universitetsforlaget, Cambrige and Oslo.

Frankfurt, H. G. (1971). Freedom of the will and the concept of a person, *The Journal of Philosophy* 68: 5–20.

Frondizi, R. (1971). *What is Value?*, Open Court Publishing Co., La Salle.

Fukuyama, F. (1989). The end of history?, *The National Interest* (16): 3–18.

Fukuyama, F. (1992). *The End of History and the Last Man*, Hamish Hamilton, London.

Gaita, R. (1991). *Good and Evil: An Absolute Conception*, Macmillan, Houndmills and London.

Galbraith, J. K. (1968). *The New Industrial State*, Mentor, New York.

Galbraith, J. K. (1987). *Economics in Perspective, A Critical History*, Houghton Mifflin Companay, Boston.

George, R. T. D. (1982). *Business Ethics*, Macmillan Publishing Co., New York.

Grenholm, C.-H. (1988). *Arbetets mening. En analys av sex teorier om arbetets syfte och värde*, Uppsala Studies in Social Ethics, Uppsala: Acta Universitatis Upsaliensis.

Grenholm, C.-H. (1993). *Protestant Work Ethics. A Study of Work in Contemporary Protestant Theology*, Uppsala Studies in Social Ethics, Uppsala: Acta Universitatis Upsaliensis.

Hacking, I. (1983). *Representing and Intervening*, Cambridge University Press, Cambridge.

Hacking, I. (1990). *The Taming of Chance*, Cambridge University Press, Cambridge.

Hausman, D. H. and McPherson, M. S. (1993). Taking ethics seriously: Economics and contemporary moral philosophy, *Journal of Economic Literature* 31: 671–731.

Hayek, F. A. (1942). Scientism and the study of society Part I, *Economica* 9: 267–291.

Hayek, F. A. (1943). Scientism and the study of society Part II, *Economica* 10: 34–63.

Hayek, F. A. (1949). *Individualism and Economic Order*, Routledge & Kegan Paul., London.

Hayek, F. A. (1967). *Studies in Philosophy, Politics and Economics.*, Routledge & Kegan Paul., London.

Hayek, F. A. (1982a). *Rules and Order, in Law, Legislation and Liberty*, Vol. 1, Routledge & Kegan Paul, London.

Hayek, F. A. (1982b). *The Mirage of Social Justice, in Law, Legislation and Liberty*, Vol. 2, Routledge & Kegan Paul, London.

Hayek, F. A. (1982c). *The Political Order of a Free People, in Law, Legislation and Liberty*, Vol. 3, Routledge & Kegan Paul, London.

Hayek, F. A. (1988). *The Fatal Conceit*, University of Chicago Press. London, Routledge., Chicago, London. The Collected Works of F. A. Hayek, Vol. 1. Edited by W. W. Bartley III.

Hayek, F. A. (1990). *New Studies in Philosophy, Politics, Economics and the History of Ideas*, Routledge & Kegan Paul., London.

Heidegger, M. (1962). Die frage nach der technik, *Die Technik und die Kehre*, Verlag Gunther Neske, Pfullingen.

Hertzberg, L. (1981). The nature of legal expertise, *in* A. Aarnio, I. Niiniluoto and J. Uusitalo (eds), *Methodologie und Erkenntnistheorie der juristischen Argumentation*, number 2 in *Rechtstheorie. Beiheft*, Duncker & Humblot, Berlin.

Hirschman, A. O. (1982). Rival interpretations of market society: Civilizing, destructive, or feeble, *Journal of Economic Literature* 20: 1463–1484.

Hodgson, G. M. (1991). Hayek's theory of cultural evolution: An evaluation in the light of Vanberg's critique, *Economics and Philosophy* 7: 67–82.

Hodgson, G. M. (1993). *Economics and Evolution. Bringing Life Back into Economics*, Polity Press, Cambridge.

Holland, R. (1980). *Against Empiricism. On Education, Epistemology and Value*, Basil Blackwell, Oxford.

Huberman, L. (1968). Man's worldly goods, the story of the wealth of nations, *Monthly Review Press* p. 158.

Jacobs, M. (1991). *The Green Economy. Environment, Sustainable Development and the Politics of the Future*, Pluto Press, London.

Jarvie, I. (1970). Understanding and explanation in sociology and social anthropology (reply to P. Winch's comment on), *in* R. Borger and F. Chioffi (eds), *Explanation in the Behavioural Sciences*, Cambridge University Press, Cambridge.

Jenkins, S. P. and Lambert, P. (1992). Ranking income distributions when needs differ. Paper presented at the 22nd conference of the Association for research on Income and Wealth.

Johnson, T. (1989). *The Voice of New Music*, Het Apollohuis, Eindhoven.

Kavanaugh, J. (1989). *Following Christ in a Consumer Society. The Spirituality of Cultural Resistance*, Orbis Books, New York.

Kortteinen, M. (1992). *Kunnian kenttä. Suomalainen palkkatyö kulttuurisena muotona*, Hanki ja Jää Oy, Hämeenlinna.

Kurtén, T. (1992). Trust, basic convictions and life-views, *Studies in Comparative Religion*, Vol. 28 of *Temenos*.

Kurtén, T. (1993). Interviews, Transcribed, mimeo, Åbo Akademi University.

Langlois, R. N. (1987). *Economics as a Process: Essays in the New Institutional Economics*, Cambridge University Press, Cambridge.

Le Grand, J. (1987). Equity, well-being and economic choice, *The Journal of Human Resources* 22(3): 429–440.

Le Grand, J. (1991). Equity as an economic objective, *in* B. Almond and D. Hill (eds), *Applied Philosophy: Morals and Metaphysics in Contemporary Debate*, Routledge, London.

Locke, J. (1965). *Two Treatises of government*, Mentor, New York.

Lodewijks, J. (1994). Anthropologists and economists: conflict or coopera-
    tion?, *Journal of Economic Methodology* 1(1): 81–104.

Löfgren, O. (1992). Mitt liv som konsument. livshistoria som forskn-
    ingsstrategi och analysmaterial, *in* C. Tigerstedt, J. Roos and A. Vilkko
    (eds), *Självbiografi, kultur, liv. Levnadshistoriska studier inom human-
    och samhällsvetenskap*, Symposion, Stockholm.

Lutz, M. (1992). Humanistic economics: history and basic principles, *in*
    P. Ekins and M. Max-Neef (eds), *Real-Life Economics. Understanding
    Wealth Creation*, Routledge, London.

Lux, K. and Lutz, M. A. (1988). *Humanistic Economics. The New Challenge*,
    Bootstrap Press, New York.

MacIntyre, A. (1990). *After Virtue. A Study in Moral Theory*, Duckworth,
    London.

Mair, D. and Miller, A. G. (1991). *A Modern Guide to Economic Thought. An
    Introduction to Comparative Schools of Thought in Economics*, Edward
    Elgar, Aldershot.

Martinez-Alier, J. (1987). *Ecological Economics. Energy, Environment and
    Society*, Basil Blackwell, Oxford.

Marx, K. (1920). *Capital. A Critical Analysis of Capitalist Production*,
    William Glaisher, Limited, London.

Marx, K. (1967). *Economic and Philosophic Manuscripts of 1844*, Inter-
    national Publishers, New York. Edited with an Introduction by D. J.
    Struik.

Mirowski, P. (1989). *More heat than light*, Cambridge University Press, Cam-
    bridge.

Moody, I. (1992). Gorecki: The path to the "Miserere", *The Musical Times*
    pp. 283–284.

Nielsen, K. (1982). Grounding rights and a method of reflective equilibrium,
    Inquiry 25: 277–306.

Nygård, F. and Sandström, A. (1981). *Measuring Income Inequality*,
    Almqvist & Wicksell International, Stockholm.

Nyman, M. (1974). *Experimental Music*, Studio Vista, London.

O'Hear, A. (1992). Criticism and tradition i Popper, Oakeshott and Hayek, *Journal of Applied Philosophy*.

Okun, A. M. (1975). *Equality and Efficiency: The Big Tradeoff*, The Brookings Institution, Washington.

O'Neill, O. (1988). Ethical reasoning and ideological pluralism, *Ethics* (98): 705–722.

Pearce, D. (1992). Economics, equity and sustainable development, *in* P. Ekins and M. Max-Neef (eds), *Real-Life Economics. Understanding Wealth Creation*, Routledge, London.

Polanyi, K. (1968). *Primitive, Archaic and Modern Economies*, Anchor Books, New York. Edited by G. Dalton.

Postel, S. (1994). Carrying capacity: Earth's bottom line, *Challenge*.

Rawls, J. (1971). *A Theory of Justice*, Clarendon Press, Oxford.

Rawls, J. (1982). Social unity and primary goods, *in* A. Sen and B. Williams (eds), *Utilitarianism and Beyond*, Cambridge University Press, Cambridge.

Rawls, J. (1993). *Political Liberalism*, Colombia University Press, New York.

Raz, J. (1980). *The Concept of a Legal System, An Introduction to the Theory of a Legal System*, 2nd ed edn, Clarendon Press, Oxford.

Raz, J. (1982). The claims of reflective equilibrium, *Inquiry* 25: 307–330.

Schumpeter, J. S. (1955). *History of Economic Analysis*, Oxford University Press, New York.

Sen, A. K. (1967). The nature and classes of prescriptive judgments, *Philosophical Quarterly* 17: 46–62.

Sen, A. K. (1973). *On Economic Inequality*, Clarendon Press, Oxford.

Sen, A. K. (1988). *On ethics and ecnomics*, Basil Blackwell, Oxford.

Sen, A. K. (1992). *Inequality Reexamined*, Clarendon, Oxford.

Sen, A. K. and Williams, B. (1982). *Utilitarianism and Beyond*, Cambridge University Press, Cambridge.

Simmel, G. (1978). *The Philosophy of Money*, Routledge & Kegan Paul., London.

Smith, A. (1976). *The Theory of Moral Sentiments*, Liberty Press, Indianapolis. Edited by Raphael, D. D. & A. L. MacFie.

Sombart, W. (1902). *Der moderne Kapitalismus*, Duncker & Humblot, Leipzig.

Stiglitz, J. (1982). Utilitarianism and horizontal equity, *Journal of Public Economics* 18: 1–33.

Stiglitz, J. E. (1993). *Economics*, W.W. Norton, New York.

Storlund, V. (1989). A searchlight on basic rights, mimeo.

Storlund, V. (1990). Social relations - a medieval appraisal, mimeo.

Storlund, V. (1992a). Public power versus industrial democracy, unpublished *Licentiate* thesis, University of Turku.

Storlund, V. (1992b). Trade union rights - what are they?, mimeo, University of Turku.

Storlund, V. (1994). Reflexive potentials in industrial relations and the law: Collective dismissal and illustration, *in* R. Rogowski and T. Wilthagen (eds), *Reflexive Labour Law*, Kluwer, Boston, MA.

Taylor, C. (1985). The nature and scope of distributive justice, *Philosophical Papers II*, Cambridge University Press, Cambridge.

Taylor, C. (1989). *Sources of the Self. The Making of the Modern Identity*, Harvard University Press, Cambridge, Massachusetts.

Tillich, P. (1951). *Systematic Theology I. Reason and Revelation. Being and God*, The University of Chicago Press, Chicago.

Tillich, P. (1963). *Systematic Theology III. Life and the Spirit. History and the Kingdom of God*, The University of Chicago Press, Chicago.

Tolonen, H. (n.d.). Normista ja oikeusnormista erityisesti John Austinin mukaan, unpublished *Licentiate* thesis, University of Turku.

Tuchman, B. W. (1979). *A Distant Mirror, The Calamitous 14th century*, Penguin Books, Harmondsworth.

Ullman-Margalit, E. (1978). Invisible-hand explanations, *Synthese* 39: 282–286.

van der Veen, R. (1991). *Between Exploitation and Communism. Explorations in the Marxian theory of justice and freedom*, Wolters-Noordhoff, Groningen.

Walker, G. (1986). *The Ethics of F. A. Hayek*, University Press of America., Lanham.

Walzer, M. (1993). *Pluralism och jämlikhet. En teori om rättvis fördelning*, Daidalos, Göteborg. English title: Spheres of Justice 1983.

Weber, M. (1923). *General Economic History*, George Allen & Unwin., London.

Weber, M. (1983). On capitalism, bureaucracy and religion, *in* S. Andreski (ed.), *Max Weber on a selection of texts*, George Allen & Unwin, London.

Weil, S. (1986). *in* S. Miles (ed.), *Simone Well: An Anthology*, Virago Press Ltd, London.

Wittgenstein, L. (1965). A lecture on ethics, *The Philosophical Review* 74: 3–12.

Wittgenstein, L. (1980). *Culture and Value*, University of Chicago Press, Chicago. translated by P.Winch.

Wolgast, E. (1992). *Ethics of an Artificial Person, Lost Responsibility in Professions and Organizations*, Stanford University Press, California.

Wong, D. B. (1984). *Moral Relativity*, University of California Press, Berkeley.

Index